Flash!

CREATE THE RIGHT FIRST IMPRESSION TO
BUILD BUZZ   CAPTURE CLIENTS   SPARK SALES

How to Market Your Company in Today's Instant World

SUSAN F. BENJAMIN

BUSINESS

AVON, MASSACHUSETTS

Published by Adams Business,
an imprint of Adams Media, a division of F+W Media, Inc.
57 Littlefield Street, Avon, MA 02322. U.S.A.
www.adamsmedia.com

ISBN 10: 1-60550-029-1
ISBN 13: 978-1-60550-029-4
eISBN 10: 1-4405-1014-8
eISBN 13: 978-1-4405-1014-4

Printed in the United States of America.

10 9 8 7 6 5 4 3 2 1

Library of Congress Cataloging-in-Publication Data
Benjamin, Susan
Flash! / Susan F. Benjamin.
p. cm.
Includes bibliographical references and index.
ISBN-13: 978-1-60550-029-4
ISBN-13: 978-1-4405-1014-4 (ebk.)
ISBN-10: 1-60550-029-1
ISBN-10: 1-4405-1014-8 (ebk.)
1. Marketing. 2. Marketing—Technological innovations. 3. Marketing—Case studies. I.
Title.
HF5415.B42917 2010

658.8—dc22
2010029130

This book is available at quantity discounts for bulk purchases.
For information, please call 1-800-289-0963.

Acknowledgments

I love the acknowledgment section of my book—it's so much fun to sit down and name names. What's most interesting is that many of the names change, but a lot of them stay the same, too.

So, in honor of the great art of redundancy, I'll start by acknowledging the names and those many people who (fortunately) don't or won't go away. First, my husband, Dan, and my son, Adam. What can I say? What can I ever say? They give me the space and humor so I can write, think, and have fun.

Then there's my agent, Grace Freedson. She's practically a sister at this point, always pulling for my career and the sprouting of new and challenging books. And she struck gold when she said "How about a book on marketing?" This book in particular has been a real pleasure to research, explore, and write.

And who could forget my proofreader, Libby Howard, who doesn't complain about my millions of typing mistakes. Thanks, Libby, for that and the details you fixed under my usual can-I-have-this-tomorrow type of deadline. Then there's Erika Ostergard, my assistant and accomplice in all sorts of buzz-related, if not inspiring, crimes. Off to the Peace Corps and new, and even more dynamic (if that's possible!), experiences.

And speaking of which—thanks to Ashley and Lissa—friends and accomplices at my marketing consulting company, Greater Voice Enterprises, and to my cohort in radio crimes, David Wolf. They gave me the opportunity to explore media from new directions—online radio and TV! It's been a wonderful experience.

As for Adams Media, thanks, Peter Archer, for the opportunity to write this book. And special thanks to all those people who directly, through interviews, or indirectly, through our work together, helped me write this book: Rich Eichwald; Richard Jernstedt; Will Sullivan; Dean Jarrett of the Martin Agency; Denell Nuese of iParty; the folks at Mori, for sending their research; Ann Vileisis, author of *Kitchen Literacy*; Ann Loehr, author of *A Manager's Guide to Coaching: Simple and Effective Ways to Get the Best Out of Your Employees*; and Maggie Macnab, author of the book *Decoding Design*, who I first interviewed for my radio show, "The Greater Voice." Also, thanks to my partner in un-marketing for a healthier you, Dr. Mark Cucuzzella. As the old saying goes . . . couldn't have done it without you!

And special thanks to Michelle Meyers for her ability to help me grow peace of mind.

Contents

Introduction: Marketing Is Everywhere

You see a book on the shelf with "marketing" in the title. Looks interesting (well, you did pick it up!) but you're wondering: is this book right for me? Undoubtedly, the answer is "Yes."

Marketing is more than efforts related to advertisements, tweets, billboards, YouTube segments, and media links from brands hoping to make a profit. Given the sea of information floating around the universe, and the limitless distractions affecting all of us, *every message is a marketing message.* In fact, you are marketing every time you:

- Apply for a job
- Advertise for a baby sitter
- Launch a brand
- Write a report
- Provide feedback to students
- Write papers for teachers   *school work, Micah*
- Present ideas at PTA meetings
- Present ideas at Rotary meetings
- Present ideas anywhere

- Work for a candidate
- Invite friends to a party
- Contact your mayor
- Discuss your small business
- Negotiate a price

Even if you do none of these things, marketing has penetrated your life; it has penetrated all our lives. This book will show how you can manage it *and* how it manages you. Remember, we're all consumers, purchasing products or services *endlessly* every day. (As long as your electricity runs, your phone works, you have Black-Berry reception, your insurance policy is current . . . you're purchasing.) Those choices about which plans you choose and brands you like are probably the result of someone else's marketing efforts. Marketing is about more than getting business: it's about how we live.

Now, here's the most stunning aspect of all: the reason we purchase items, believe in causes, choose politicians, and select services has less to do with what we *think* about them than how we *feel* about them emotionally, physically, viscerally. This connection works quickly, taking less than a fraction of a second to launch. In other words, it happens in a flash.

Are we aware we're responding this way? Aware of the other implications of these messages on our lives? Or of the flash triggered by our own heartfelt communications? Heck, no. Which is precisely why the whole subject is so enlightening, empowering, and well worth knowing about.

More about Flash

The first time I confronted the idea of flash, I was reading Ellen Langer's book *Mindfulness*. In it, Dr. Langer, a professor in the

Psychology Department at Harvard University, discussed how humans often respond to messages without thinking: a response that's automatic, etched into our psychic muscle. We look in the rearview mirror when we're about to turn or put our foot on the brake if a car in front of us abruptly stops. These unthinking responses are necessary: if we stopped to think before doing any of them, we could jeopardize our lives. Besides, life entails so many actions every moment of the day, it's simply not possible to think about all of them.

We don't always respond in ways that are helpful to us. Think about walking along a busy street in a place like Manhattan. You see a "Going out of Business" sign in a store window. Without thinking, you enter the shop, where a sales representative is waiting to greet you. A few minutes later, you walk out with a newly purchased product you never intended to get and probably don't need. The sign triggered a response that was as familiar and unintentional as putting a foot to the brake.

According to Dr. Langer, if you give the sale some thought, you might reconsider your purchase. Do you need that product? Do you have enough money to spend? Besides, that store is always going out of business—every store goes out of business eventually. And even if this particular store *is* tanking, that's no reason to shop there— possibly quite the opposite.

What's pivotal about Langer's views is the question, "What *particular* aspect of the communication ignited the response in the first place?" This is the problem I set out to explore: Why do people respond to messages? Is it the word use? The venue? I had many opportunities to address these questions, thanks to my corporate clients and the federal agencies I worked for as part of a Clinton/ Gore White House initiative on Plain Language.

What became clear to me was that in all messages, regardless of content, the way the message was articulated triggered the audience's response. A store sign that read "Sale! Today only! 50% off EVERYTHING!" would be significantly more compelling than one that read, "We are having a sale and will be selling all our merchandise at half-off. The sale will only last for the day, though."

Around that time I conducted a study in which a control group of candidates for federal jobs looked at sample vacancy announcements that had long paragraphs, thick with ink. The candidates had trouble understanding the announcements and thought the employer was being difficult, unfriendly, trying to put blocks in the way of their success. Then, with another group, we broke the text into shorter paragraphs (without changing the content). The candidates had an easier time understanding the message and felt significantly more positive about applying.

Gradually, over time, more findings started drifting in from sources everywhere:

- Visitors form an impression of a website in less time than it takes to blink.
- Messaging creates associations and fuels memories we aren't aware we're experiencing.
- Specific words and images trigger responses deep in our brain such as fear, trust, or sexiness.
- Once that flash is triggered, it colors the way we perceive the website, brand, or product. Quite possibly that perspective never goes away. This is called the "halo" effect.

Effective marketers know how to manage flash to maximize the response they get from the audience. Does this mean flash is some-

FLASH = automatic response

how sneaky? Evil? Outrageous? As marketers, should we remove flash elements from our own marketing campaigns?

That's impossible—even if I thought it was necessary. Flash is an organic event; it's how we respond to messages—we *always* respond instantly. An e-mail at work creates flash. A text message about a party creates flash. Even a note left on a kitchen table in the morning can create flash.

Marketers carefully study their demographics and develop strategies to trigger the most advantageous flash response. Feelings of risk, wildness, and deviance will work for an adolescent male but probably not his boomer grandmother. Not all flash is predictable or beneficial to the marketer. Just as bad, some is ineffective. In other words, the flash doesn't go off.

The relevance of flash—and the attention paid to it—has skyrocketed as the number of marketing and media messages the audience receives has soared from a few hundred or so a week a few decades ago to anywhere from 5,000 to 7,000 *a day*. Cereal companies send them. So do government officials, drug manufacturers, school systems, book peddlers, clinics, psychologists, hairdressers, yoga teachers, and religious organizations marketing their orientation to God. The sheer volume of such messages makes marketing the *single strongest cultural influence* in our society today.

CALL IN THE CLERGY . . .

Marketing messages are subliminal and powerful. But something more is on-hand: With the Internet, marketing messages can reach more people (thousands within nanoseconds) for longer periods of time (you can't erase messages in cyberspace) than ever in history. Today marketers have also greater access to the tools that generate flash and motivate responses, including neuromarketing, which is a practice using magnetic resonance imaging (MRIs) to determine how messaging affects the brain.

This results in one resounding fact: you can't discuss marketing without addressing ethical issues. These range from whether it's right to have friends endorse your brand in the comments section of your blog to whether it's wrong to "mislead" the public about the health benefits of a food. We'll look at these issues throughout the book with plenty of examples that illustrate, and push, the point.

THE ONLY CONSTANT IS CHANGE

Flash can't exist without vehicles to channel it, whether websites, social networks, or good old-fashioned word of mouth. Yet, these vehicles, and the strategies necessary to work within them, change constantly, fueled by technology, the global economy, scientific findings about behavior, and the emerging mentality of the audience. The changes are fascinating and unexpected, the possibilities boundless. Ancient history has gone from being years in the past to a few weeks ago. Plenty of people think they have The Answer. But, trust me, they don't. The Answer comes and goes in a moment.

Consider YouTube. It's integral to our online life, whether you're a strategic marketer or surfer looking for something cool. Yet YouTube is young, a baby—it was only founded in 2005 and brought into the limelight when Google purchased it in 2006.

As for Google, it was founded by Stanford students, incorporated in 1998, and the initial public offering took place a mere six years later, in 2004. In that short time, it went from a concept to a part of the global universe—so integral that the noun "Google" has also become a verb.

With all these changes, with all the blogs, tweaks, geeks, neuromarketing, and sensory strategies, the only thing that's likely to remain the same is flash.

What's Ahead

In the following chapters, we'll discuss the many aspects of flash and how it applies to marketing today and tomorrow. We'll include information about how marketers use it; how you can leverage it; and how if affects our lives. Throughout the chapters, you'll also find tips for those of you On the Front Lines, who create marketing materials every day. You'll learn how to apply these ideas for powerful, creative, and honest results. Then, at the end of every chapter, there is a checklist you can use to shape your campaign.

PART 1

IN THE BEGINNING: A FLASH OF LIGHT

You must market !

1. Flash What?

Marketing is everything. It's everywhere. It's a major force in our culture and, like it or hate it, it's here to stay. If you want to get word out about your product, service, idea, or even yourself (think Facebook), you must market. For success, though, you must embrace the constant yet ever-changing nature of messaging.

Think of a swift-flowing river, on which you paddle a canoe every few months. You may think you know its course pretty well. But each time you paddle it, it's changed slightly. And if you neglect it for, say, a year, you'll find that it's changed completely. You'll also find that this particular river is flowing just a bit faster each time you paddle it. Thus, it's changing at an ever-increasing pace.

Thanks to advances in technology, changes in marketing are also speeding up. Today's marketers can draw on research into such topics as how the brain receives and processes information, the amount of information that's thrust into the world every second, and, in an ironic twist, the power of marketers to get word out about their own marketing strategies. All this movement, every demand, is wrapped around a single concept: flash.

Flash Marketing: The Definition

Think of the word "flash." It's all about immediacy. Speed. Energy. You experience flash throughout the day—it's simply how you process information. When you smell something, such as a pot of coffee in the morning, you immediately take notice at a gut level, even before your brain registers the thought, "Mmmm, that smells good!" It hits you in a preconscious flash, before you're consciously aware that you noticed. That flash is deep, tapping into feelings, memories, and associations.

Flash: The Definition

By saying "flash" we mean:

- Our response to messages—it's quick, at a visceral, preconscious level.
- The quality of your message, which enables it to yield those results.

Flash is about more than that, though. It's about why we react to some messages and not others. About the secret "lessons" embedded in those messages, independent of the product, service, or idea the marketer is promoting. And, it's about a mirror that reflects who we are. It's about several other things as well.

FLASH MEMORY

The audience may have a flash response to the message, but marketers need to reinforce that flash response consistently. Otherwise the audience, blitzed with other messages, may forget, in their brains and their physical selves. For example, read these brand names:

- Godiva Chocolate
- Hershey's Chocolate
- Cocoa Puffs

Through the longevity of the brands (the Hershey Company was founded in 1894), the extent of their market, their continued presence in your life (even to a small degree), probably have specific feelings, with associations, connected to each of them. Godiva is refined, elegant, expensive, and romantic. Hershey's is fun, accessible, tasty, familiar. As for Cocoa Puffs: they're goofy, guilt-inducing (for adults), and familiar. You may think: Ah-ha! I *remember* Cocoa Puffs from when I was a kid. More likely, though, you experience the memory—a blend of smell, color, and, above all, feeling—which occurs at remarkable speed. So remarkable, in fact, you may not be aware you're experiencing it.

The flash memory incorporates many things, including your experience of the brand. For example, when I was a kid, I had chickenpox. For some reason, my mother let me have Pop-Tarts for breakfast, a treat I wasn't allowed to have any other time. I remember eating them in front of television, feeling slightly warm and itchy. When I see Pop-Tarts today, the feeling of comfort, security, and even pleasure return, although the sickness is a vague and unremarkable occurrence in my life.

Marketers play an enormous role in shaping that flash. They may introduce or reintroduce the product. They send repeated messages, involving music, images, and smells. And they link the brand to your values. Cheerios today is all about low cholesterol because that's what their demographic of health-conscious professionals wants. In the past, it was the energy cereal ("Big 'G' Little 'o,' Go with Cheerios"), and could easily be a diet food (think Special K).

Similarly, marketers could have positioned Cocoa Puffs as an elegant treat for brunches or evening desserts and Godiva as a sweet treat for busy Moms on the go. But they didn't. Such positioning, in fact, strikes us as ridiculous . . . but that's the result of our own flash memory experiences.

rily reach its audience directly, but passes to ople who spread it in their daily conversa- s. The way they articulate their thoughts, nat in which they do so, will affect the audi- . In such cases, the driver is not the brand, but rather whoever is discussing it.

INVISIBLE FLASH

Constant Contact's logo at the bottom of an e-newsletter. A tag that says "CK" on it. A sponsor's name on public radio. The flash may be there, but do you notice? Does the association between public radio and the sponsor register at all? Not until you confront the brand directly. You don't remember seeing or hearing the name, but there's a flash of familiarity. At some level, you know.

Marketers tap the senses to create that flash experience: the more senses, the richer the flash. Here's a look at some of them:

Sight

An image, whether a symbol, a building, or a person, can trigger a flash, whether sympathy, humor, or excitement. Maggie Macnab, author of the book *Decoding Design*, a fascinating look at the symbolic meaning of business images, explained to me that our response to strong designs "crosses cultures and eras with symbols, shapes and forms that relate to patterns in the universe that we all recognize at an intuitive level."

She points to these examples from the business world:

- **"Target** The target represents focus, perfecting your aim, and hitting whatever mark is in front of you, whether catching prey or reaching professional goals. The company Target adopted the three-ringed target in the 60s but has since narrowed it down to a single ring surrounding another, also indicating one encircled by all.

- **"Vesica Pisces.** The Vesica Pisces, or two overlapping circles that create a third shape, was common in Gothic architecture and manuscripts in the Middle Ages. It mirrors cellular division when life comes into being and represents duality in the world. One example: the MasterCard logo. The Eastern version of duality is represented by the yin-yang symbol, now commonly seen in our culture. This symbol addresses integration and balance as well, as you can see from the image.

- **"Triangle.** No mere shape we learned to draw in grammar school, the triangle has a deeply intuitive connotation, representing how life exists: we come into being, we live, and we die. So, where do we see this symbol? Perfectly displayed on recycling signs." Macnab points out that the universe contains a finite number of shapes used as building blocks in the construction of these designs—the circle, square, spiral, cross, and triangle. The designer's job is to identify the shape that is right for your business and embed it with specific information for a powerful flash reaction.

Smell

Marketers in the food and beverage industry know this well. Some bakers use fans to blow the scent of freshly baked breads and cakes from the stoves to the lobby and out the door. No doubt Starbucks owes at least some of its success to the coffee smell that immediately hits you when you walk in the door. You smell it and instantly your body, your emotions, your *gut* responds, even before you register that you want it.

However, something more is going on. According to marketing expert Lucas Conley, 75 percent of our everyday emotions are influenced by smell. So marketers *outside* the food industry, especially big-budget marketers, are using scent as a way to promote their products and make a deep, enduring impression on the consumer.

One example that Conley sites in his book *Obsessive Branding Disorder* is Auracell: a plastic material made by a company called Rotuba. Unlike other plastics, which smell unpleasant, or neutral at best, Auracell can hold one of 33,000 fragrances for up to three months. That makes it useful to companies like Unilever, which is releasing a sweet-smelling bottle for its Suave shampoo, and Huggies, which is crawling toward a scented diaper. There are also cologne-scented golf tees, lavender-scented cell phones, mimosa-scented bangles, and scented caps on lip balm, targeting tweens. Some video stores even exude a butter-flavored scent, and supermarkets plant fruit-punch scented coupon dispenses to lure parents—and children—to Motrin.

Granted, scent marketing has a frightening Big Brother quality to it, making the days when consumers worried about subliminal messages slipping into their advertising seem like a cozy memory. Currently few companies are using scent marketing in their campaigns; the majority still rely on reaching the audience from a *visual* standpoint.

So, what does this tell you, as a marketer? That scent marketing can be a viable, highly effective part of your campaign but, like every new strategy, has plenty of opportunity to mislead the audience. Think of the old days when department store salesgirls sprayed perfume on the customer's wrist to entice her into buying their product. It was annoying and often triggered allergic reactions in the people it was supposed to be enticing.

Words

You cannot underestimate the depth and significance words convey and the immediacy of their effect. Like images and sounds, they have deep significance within our culture. For example, "up" is a positive word: the stock market is "up," we feel "up" after hearing good news, and a vitamin drink is "uplifting." What's most critical to remember, though, is that words get their power, their flash quality, by working on *highly* metaphorical levels. The stock market, our feelings, and the drink aren't literally going into space. Our culture just agrees that "up" is good, and that using the word triggers good feelings.

By using words strategically, acutely aware of how your demographic responds to them, you can create deep and ultimately enduring flash. Here are two examples that illustrate the point:

"Take the Special K Challenge and drop a jean size in two weeks."

The flashpoint of this sentence comes at the word "drop." "Drop" has energy and power. You drop a glass and it shatters. You drop a hundred dollars and you spent a lot. You can *feel* the word, experience it, with all the metaphorical value that it brings. Do you literally drop the pounds? Even the question is bizarre. Now, notice the difference in these examples:

- Take the Special K Challenge and come down a jean size in two weeks.
- Take the Special K Challenge and get rid of a jean size in two weeks.
- Take the Special K Challenge and lower your jean size in two weeks.

The flash just isn't there.

Marketers, especially food marketers, focus on women with a ferocity normally equated with college students and sex. Women are easy targets, as they make 80 percent of spending decisions in the United States and make an even larger percentage of decisions about food. Besides, women are perennially concerned with their looks, especially their weight.

So, marketers, like the ones behind Special K's messaging, promise women a slimmer self with words that generally focus on diminishing size, such as "slim down," "lose inches," and "cut calories." Given the great proliferation of diet-based marketing, it's possible that marketing created the need for diets in the first place. Without marketers, women might focus on the quality of their food, not the calorie count or the lifestyle of their families, which may be what leads to a weight problem in the first place. But how can you sell lifestyle changes and still make a profit?

Besides, 95 percent of dieters regain their weight within three years, making diet foods a gift that keeps on giving. The flash never dims.

My advice: If you're going to use words to trigger flash, be sure you mean it.

"[Grape Nut's] *taste reminds me of* wild hickory nuts."

That's according to Euell Gibbons, the famed naturalist, in an immensely popular ad campaign that reigned in the 1970s. Everything about the word use here underscores the power of words on an *entirely* symbolic level. Think of the feelings conjured by the name "Grape Nuts." Two healthy foods, grapes and nuts, brought together in one cereal name. It *has* to conjure feelings of health, well-being, security, and trust.

The point, though, is this: There's no such thing as a grape nut. Not in nature and not, I must add, in the Grape Nuts box. The cereal bits, which resemble grains of sand on steroids, are made of flour cooked to a density rarely seen in the natural world. Similarly, who has ever eaten a wild hickory nut? Or, for that matter, ever heard of a wild hickory nut? But the words trigger a flash response that defies all reason and made Grape Nuts the seventh-leading cereal at the time.

One *Wall Street Journal* article quotes senior brand manager Carin Gendell as saying her staff claimed, "Grape Nuts was people eating advertising."

Sound

The flash possibilities of sound, especially music, are more obvious than words or images. Good jingles, for example, evoke specific and instantaneous feelings. The audience may *feel* the rhythms or hear it in their heads, later. In many cases, the audience needs to hear the jingle only *once* to remember it. The list ranges from old-timers like the McDonald's jingle "You deserve a break today . . ." to Kay Jewelers' "Every kiss begins with Kay."

Interestingly, sound can function *best* when the audience isn't aware that they're hearing it. Once example we'll discuss soon is direct advertising icon Billy Mays. Think about it. The audience could remember how he sounded, and what he was pitching, more or less. But do you remember the background music on his ads? It was as buoyant and innocent as the music of a merry-go-round and contributes to the flash effect. When he died in 2009, Mays had changed the direct mail universe and the audience grieved his passing.

FLASH FOR YOU: Flash huh?

If you're marketing on a limited budget without access to tools such as MRIs, you can still apply the principles of flash to your campaign. The overriding concept here is authenticity. Focus on the value of your brand, not something you feel compelled to concoct or manipulate, and on the feeling that suits it best. Marketing efforts for scary movies (think jiggered, severed fingers in the posters for *Saw*) create a flash experience of fear.

Neuromarketing: Where Flash Meets MRIs

While everyone from traveling snake-oil salesmen to modern politicians have used flash, albeit unknowingly, to win over their audience, today's marketers are exploring new ways to harness its power.

In his book *Buy-ology*, marketing expert Martin Lindstrom discusses new research about how the brain responds to marketing messages. For example, a message triggering excitement will motivate people not only to *buy*, but buy immediately. Those immediate emotional responses, he points out, have a strong physical component. With excitement the audience may experience sweaty palms or a quickening heartbeat. Although these sensations may be small, even unnoticeable on a conscious level, they exist.

But marketers aren't content with observing how messages work or receiving subjective feedback through surveys or tests; they want to get inside the audiences' brain to know precisely how the audience is responding. Enter neuromarketing. Developed by Gary Zaltman of Harvard University in the 1990s, neuromarketing is a marketing research tool using imaging diagnostics such as Magnetic Resonance Imaging (MRI) or Quantified Electroencephalography (QEEE). With it, marketers can tell what parts of the brain become activated by smells, images, sounds, and other components of a marketing campaign.

According to Max Sutherland, author of the book *Advertising and the Mind of the Consumer*, "Brain *wave* recording devices have been available for decades but new technology can now pinpoint more precisely which brain regions are active as people respond to products or make brand choices or are exposed to advertisements. The neuroscience dream of being able to peer into the functioning brain has been made possible."

Here are a few examples:

- When DaimlerChrysler measured brainwave activity with an fMRI scanner, they found that images of sports cars stimulated the reward center of the brain, the same one that responds to drugs, alcohol, and sex. The headlights triggered a response in the facial recognition part of the brain, which activates such feelings as trust.
- Frito-Lay recognized that women are more prone to guilt than are men, women eat more snack food than do men, and Frito-Lay was losing share in the woman's market. To reach women, they needed to make them feel guilt-free, or at least less guilty, about eating Frito-Lay products. According to Forbes, "Executives . . . discovered that matte beige bags of potato chips picturing potatoes and other 'healthy' ingredients in the snack don't trigger activity in the anterior cingulate cortex—an area of the brain associated with feelings of guilt—as much as shiny bags with pictures of chips. Frito-Lay then switched out of shiny packaging in the U.S. . . . ."

Most amazing of all the recent findings is that marketing can actually change how the consumer *experiences* the product. As you can probably guess, one flash point is price. If you see a bottle of wine marked $10 and one marked $25, you'll naturally believe that the more expensive bottle is better. Antonio Rangel, an associate professor at the California Institute of Technology, wanted to test this idea. According to a Caltech release, Rangel and his team found "that changes in the stated price of a sampled wine influenced not only how good volunteers thought it tasted, but the activity of a brain region that is involved

Price

in our experience of pleasure. In other words, 'prices, by themselves, affect activity in an area of the brain that is thought to encode the experienced pleasantness of an experience,' Rangel says."

Also involved in the study was Baba Shiv, an associate professor of marketing at Stanford Graduate School of Business. According to Stanford reports, "studies have shown that marketing can influence how people value goods. For example, Shiv has shown that people who paid a higher price for an energy drink, such as Red Bull, were able to solve more brain teasers than those who paid a discounted price for the same product."

FLASH FOR YOU: What's the trigger?

It's difficult for even the most astute marketers to control the flash response they get from their messaging. So, your best option is to align the components of your messaging as closely as possible with your brand. Energy drinks targeting adolescents have energizing names like Rockstar and images of stars that practically burst from the can.

The Feeling Brain

Research into neuroscience tells us that emotion is actually part of our brain's functioning, playing a pivotal role in how we make any decision. In his book *How We Decide*, Jonah Lehrer explains that "the process of thinking requires feeling, for feelings are what let us understand all the information that we can't directly comprehend. Reason without emotion is impotent."

He describes an extreme example of decision-making involving baseball players, saying:

> A typical major league pitch takes about 0.35 seconds to travel from the hand of the pitcher to home plate. (This is the average

interval between human heartbeats.) Unfortunately for the batter, it takes about 0.25 seconds for his muscles to initiate a swing, leaving his brain a paltry one-tenth of a second to make up its mind on whether or not to do so . . . the batter really has fewer than five milliseconds to perceive the pitch and decide if he should swing. But people can't think this quickly.

Lehrer tells us the batter knows when to bat because his brain can convert knowledge into feeling: "A hanging curve ball over the plate just *feels* like a better pitch than a slider, low and away."

Marketers are able to trigger that feeling at lightning speed. The glow may last for a long time, or never disappear, thanks to something known as the halo effect.

The Halo Effect

The halo effect is exactly what it sounds like: the initial flash leaves a halo around the message and the brand that is extremely hard to lose. With websites, for example, the audience responds to the first webpage they encounter in less time than they take to blink. Whatever impression they initially experienced will color their response in subsequent pages. In a sense, the halo effect is just another way of saying, "First impressions are lasting impressions."

But the halo effect isn't restricted to marketing copy: it can affect all the marketing efforts. Remember that wine study we looked at earlier? In a related experiment at the University of Illinois, students went to a relatively upscale restaurant on campus. When they were seated, the waiter told them they were getting a free glass of Cabernet. One group of guests was told they were getting a California wine while the others would receive a North Dakota wine. Actually, both groups received Charles Shaw Cabernet Sauvignon.

Now, here's where the halo effect came in: the students who drank the presumably superior California wine (have you ever heard of a good North Dakota wine?) thought more highly of the food and ate more of it.

Anatomy of Flash

That initial, preconscious feeling triggers other responses that make the flash experience complete. Here is a quick look at what follows:

1. *Initial flash.* This is the preconscious stage we've been discussing. The message gets into your audience's nervous system, into their blood, muscle, and memory.
2. *Context.* The audience contextualizes the message. The bag of chips is from Frito-Lay and it's new.
3. *Understanding.* You can also call this stage "knowing" or "grasping" the message. With Frito-Lay, the audience understands the company has added a new line to its inventory that's healthy, low in cholesterol, and otherwise guilt-free.
4. *Action.* The audience purchases the brand, but only if their excitement has peaked and the situation is right. Marketers infuse their campaigns with motivators: sales that end in three days; limited numbers of products; exclusive offers *you can get nowhere else*; promises that the audience will be the *first* to use it. The flash experience of excitement and anxiety is intense and the audience acts. Do they actually need the brand? Would they have made the purchase without these motivators? You can probably guess the answer to that.

Typically, though, the audience becomes familiar with the brand after repeated, consistent experiences. Only then, under the right circumstances, do they spring into action.

Flash Case Study 1: Let's Go, Flash

Direct-response advertising is a great example of one-hit wonders: the flash experience is strong enough for the audience to respond immediately. And no one was quite as successful as the late Billy Mays, who pitched everything from self-watering planters to miracle hair removal kits. Billy opened his ads with "Billy Mays here, . . ." and he wore every-guy chinos and an oxford shirt. As we discussed earlier, his voice was excited but reassuring, the background music reminiscent of what plays on merry-go-rounds. The flash experience was about urgency and trust, reinforced in every ad.

The audience responds this way:

1. Flash response. Excitement, trust, longing, joy.
2. Context. This is an exciting offer.
3. Understanding. I can get all this stuff for $19.99 but only if I call right away.
4. Action. The audience calls.

The flash response basically cancels out rational thinking, including whether the viewers actually need the miracle hair removal kit (and whether it's a miracle, anyway) and whether they really do need to get it right then or lose it forever. And, they don't ask, don't even *think* to ask, how the company is making its money. The answer: by selling its information to other marketers for lots of money.

FLASH FOR YOU: An urgent flash

While Billy Mays–style marketing may have dubious intent (although high entertainment value for some), creating a flash response of urgency isn't a bad thing, either. During the earthquake in Haiti, for example, fundraisers wanted people throughout the world to send money quickly. Every day could cost lives, and triggering a flash response of urgency was key. Don't call about it. Don't consult with your CPA. Just send. If you're introducing a new product or service, urgency will break the audience out of their complacency and heighten the likelihood they'll try something new.

Flash Case Study 2: The Mac Flash

In the Apple Computer ads, the audience sees actor Justin Long, dressed in jeans and an un-tucked oxford, with stylishly longish hair, as trustworthy as the singer Jackson Browne was in his youth. He says: "Hello, I'm a Mac." Beside him, we see chubby and pale John Hodgman in a nerdy suit and glasses. He's the PC. In one ad he sits in front of a bake sale table trying to raise money to fix the famously flawed Vista product. In another he wears a biohazard suit to fight off a virus. The Mac guy is coolly unconvinced.

The audience responds this way:

- Flash response. Pleasantly off-balance (the prelude to humor).
- Context. Ah—this is a Mac ad.
- Understanding. The Mac is hip, the PC isn't. Depending on their exposure to the ad and buzz about it, the audience gets it that Hodgmen portrays Bill Gates and Justin Long, Steve Jobs.
- Action. Any of these actions (and others) would work: The audience talks about the ad, creating buzz; goes online to learn more; buys a Mac; switches from PC to Mac relatively soon or months or even years after; feels good about the next series of ads. You can see the series on *www.apple.com/getamac/ads*.

Flash That Flopped

Exxon has a suite of eco-friendly marketing campaigns. In one advertisement for liquefied natural gas, for example, Exxon employees, who look like they've just spent the weekend in a nature preserve, discuss the eco-benefits of the company's products. The backdrop is sparkling white and as hazard-free as an intensive care unit. Yet, no matter how the audience initially responds to the ad, the Exxon brand, shaped in large part by the company's history, is a deal killer, and the ad just isn't effective. In fact, the United Kingdom's Advertising Standards Authority banned it. It's just too easy for the audience to call to mind two fatal words: *Exxon Valdez.*

Some marketing takes the audience though part of the flash process and leaves them hanging. In promos, for example, movie and television marketers reveal a sharp image, such as a villainous face or a hysterically screaming character, eliciting a flash of excitement, curiosity, fear. The voiceover says: "Coming This Fall." The audience has the context but not the understanding. *What* is coming this fall? The unresolved thoughts and feeling create a longer, more sustained involvement from the audience, which learns what the movie's about later.

Another example is Cartoon Network's marketing campaign, headed by creative agency Interference, Inc. The agency intended to generate buzz for its client's upcoming movie, *Aqua Teen Hunger Force.* So it created electronic devices about half the size a of a baking pan, with a robot-looking figure giving the finger to passersby. The marketers attached these figures to spots throughout Boston, New York City, Los Angeles, Chicago, Atlanta, Seattle, Portland, Austin, San Francisco, and Philadelphia, including the sides of bridges, with *no* indication of what they were.

In other words, they got to the gut-response (surprise, excitement, and curiosity) level and possibly to the second level of context (a weird shape attached to the side of the bridge), but left the audience *not* understanding why the device was there or what they were supposed to do about it. Their expectation was that people would buzz about it and build suspense, which would be relived when they announced the movie. Unfortunately, the flash response

Flash Memory = 5 Flashes

in the Boston crowd was fear, even panic. Residents misinterpreted the effort for a bomb scare and Homeland Security was called in.

Love at Fifth Sight: The Irony of Flash

The irony of flash is that audiences usually need a repeated flash experience for it to become flash memory. The marketing world calls this "Love at Fifth Sight." It takes at least five times for the audience to remember, trust, and essentially own the brand. The more varied the exposure—radio interviews, YouTube presence, articles, blogs by and about the brand, and buzz from others—and the more consistent the messaging, the more likely they'll succeed.

FLASH FOR YOU: Price checks

What about budget? You may be intimidated about the enormity and expense of a marketing campaign, particularly if you work for a cause, not-for-profit, or small business, especially your own. So here are some ways to leverage the possibilities of marketing, without the expense:

Invest in thought time. The real significance of any effort is the thought that goes into it. So, plan to spend time looking at all aspects of your campaign.

Look for freeware. Technology plays an enormous part in most marketing campaigns. Depending on your business, the online universe is simply too big and important for you to ignore. But there's plenty of technology out there that's free, or close to it. To learn more, you can search the Internet or hire someone to explain.

Learn from other people's successes. Go to the Word of Mouth Marketing Association's website, *www.womma.org*, and read its case studies. Then go to other websites of marketing, PR, and communications firms and read their case studies. They'll help you identify ways of triggering discussion long after your initial messaging is out.

CHAPTER 1:

Flash! Review

Flash is how people naturally process information. The immediate flash will create a halo effect that will color your message and possibly your brand—for better or worse. The flash experience should be directly connected to the feeling the audience gets from your brand.

Your marketing message must have these qualities:

- Engage the audience, don't simply address them.
- Be consistent over the long term.
- Tap as many of the audience's senses (audio, visual, scent, touch) as possible.

Your message must be authentic or it will not work. The audience responds more to "how you say it" than "what you say." Still, you must be honest at all times, regardless of how tempting a misleading message may be.

2. Brand in a Flash

For many in the marketing universe, the concept of brand is an enigma. Is brand a logo and design? A way of packaging products? Or the appearance embedded in a marketing campaign? The answer is "yes" to all of the above. Brand is the personality of a business, idea, even a social cause, and it is expressed in everything they do. The Republicans have their brand—so do Democrats. The green movement has a brand, but so does Wal-Mart. If a company doesn't have a clear, easily identifiable brand, it's invisible. The brand must be reflected in everything, including:

- **Language**—from an ad to a customer service letter
- **Design**—from marketing materials to the website policy page
- **Physical location**—including lobby, signs, and the building's interior
- **Online presence**—such as blogs, webpages, and videos posted on YouTube
- **Employees**—in their approach to phone services, help desks, online assistance, and each other

The Brand-Flash Connection

If "brand" is the personality of a company, product, or even grass-roots movement, the flash is how we feel about it. The two must be consistent or the message will have no effect or will backfire.

Think about Martha Stewart. She is the brand and she inspires flash feelings of confidence, warmth, and order. Okay, some people might think, "Huh? Confidence? Warmth?" My husband, who works for the Marines, is definitely one of them. But he is *not* Martha's demographic, so who cares.

The Martha Stewart brand is also remarkably consistent: Everything she does, from her magazine to her television show, reinforces that initial flash.

One of my clients recounted a meeting between Stewart and representatives of a marketing firm who hoped to win her business. Ms. Stewart showed up with polite, well-coiffed assistants who served the participants slices of black walnut cake. Ms. Stewart waited until everyone tasted their slice to ensure they enjoyed it, described where the black walnuts grew and what made them so perfect for the recipe, and offered them more.

That consistency was helpful in 2004 when Ms. Stewart was sentenced to five months in prison for lying about investments. At the time, reporters, fans, and most certainly detractors (including some of her employees) believed this was the end of the multimillion-dollar homemaker. Although they didn't say it, they believed the flash had shifted: audiences would experience negative flash when confronted with her brand.

Yet, the audience (and investors) welcomed Stewart back once she was released. The flash was too deeply entrenched, too consistently reinforced, to be anything but solid. According to one MSNBC report, when Stewart first arrived in prison she said that "she will miss her pets during her stay in prison, but hoped to be free in time for spring gardening." Her brand was *that* consistent.

Deeply embedded flash can also harm a brand that's longing to change. Exxon, which I mentioned earlier, is one example. The company's advertising campaigns tried to create a flash experience of trust, familiarity, and comfort. Yet, the flash that Exxon has been generating for too long is too negative.

Another example is the 2008 election. Times were tough for the Republicans. President George W. Bush had reached record lows in his popularity, the war in Iraq had in no way met anyone's expectations, and the president's mantra was about staying the course. Enter the Obama campaign. Their flashpoint was about energy, newness, and hope, pivoting around the word "change." It also promised relief from the prevailing feelings of anger, insecurity, fear, and exhaustion.

John McCain tried to integrate "change" into his campaign. According to one *Huffington Post* article:

> On Tuesday, the Senator co-opted the slogan that has come to personify Obama's candidacy, taking the Illinois Democrat's "Change You Can Believe In" and altering it into "A Leader You Can Believe In."

> The line adorned McCain's lime-green backdrop as he addressed supporters in Louisiana. During that speech, moreover, the Arizonan took his Obama-posing a step further, uttering the word "change" more than 30 times. Not that Obama can claim sole ownership of the word or idea, but still . . . .

The article also points out that McCain co-opted Obama's logo and color scheme, using similar shades of red and blue. The strategy failed: McCain, a Bush Republican entrenched in politics-as-usual, could not overcome the flash his brand triggered. Ironically,

McCain's campaign had crafted that image carefully, leaving behind the former "maverick" brand that was the hallmark of McCain's previous marketing efforts.

When Brand Meets Metaphor

Plenty of marketers create flash responses by using metaphors. These are incredibly helpful and complex, as one image, one word, can trigger numerous, deeply held beliefs, feelings, and associations.

One example is Häagen Daz ice cream. The original owners were Reuben and Rose Mattus, Polish immigrants living in New York. They decided on a name that would serve as a symbol of richness, sophistication, northern European charm. So, they invented "Häagen Daz," made up of two nonexistent Scandinavian-sounding words. That was in 1961. Now owned by Pillsbury, the ice cream's name still triggers a flash of elegance and pleasure, supported by other brand elements: the names of particular flavors, the package, the ingredients list.

Metaphors can stretch the lines of truth. The founders of Quaker Oats, for example, were among the first to seize the concept of brand at the end of the nineteenth century. They named their product after the Society of Friends, or Quakers, who had a reputation for hard work, purity, and honesty. The name and the logo of a smiling, old-fashioned Quaker ignite a flash of trust and reliability. Today, Quaker Oats is owned by PepsiCo, Inc. and prevails as the nation's leading oatmeal.

Yet the connection between Quaker Oats and the actual Society of Friends is nonexistent. Ironically, the actual Society of Friends are ardent truth-tellers and not happy with the packaged oats.

Another example from the supermarket aisles is Yoplait yogurt. The company, based in France, is franchised in the United States by General Mills. The logo is a flower—a metaphor for wholesomeness, freshness, and goodness . . . and it's everywhere on the company's website, product labels, and ads. Yogurt in general triggers a flash experience of healthiness and security; the Yoplait metaphor reinforces it. But how honest is the metaphor? Take a look at the ingredients panel on the strawberry variety:

> *Cultured Pasteurized Grade A Low Fat Milk, Sugar, Strawberries, Modified Corn Starch, High Fructose Corn Syrup, Nonfat Milk, Kosher Gelatin, Citric Acid, Tricalcium Phosphate, Natural Flavor, Pectin, Colored with Carmine, Vitamin A Acetate, Vitamin D3.*

On his website, "Fooducate," blogger Hemi Weingarten points out that:

> *The front of the yogurt label boldly claims it is 99% fat-free, leading a person to expect a very low calorie yogurt. Instead, 170 calories. Not a lot, but not close to zero either . . . . Note though, that 108 of these 170 calories are from sugar! In context . . . 63% of the calories in Yoplait Strawberry Yogurt are from sugar!*

Common sense tells us that flower or not, Yoplait is hardly about nature. As its website tells us, its other flavors include:

Banana Crème, Mountain Blueberry, Boysenberry, Cherry Orchard, French Vanilla, Harvest Peach, Key Lime Pie, Mandarin Orange, Mixed Berry, Orange Crème, Pineapple, Red Raspberry, Strawberry, Strawberry Banana, Strawberry Cheesecake, Strawberry Kiwi, Strawberry Mango, Tropical Peach, White Chocolate Raspberry, Harvest Blackberry, Blueberry Crumble, Peach Cobbler, Berry Banana

Unless I'm mistaken, crème, cheesecake, and Key lime pie don't grow in the flower-speckled fields of France. But, as we've underscored, consumers don't necessarily make decisions based on thought, and it's up to marketers to treat them honestly.

FLASH FOR YOU: Headin' for heaven
Of course, you don't have to be honest to make your campaign work. Many businesses (not to mention politicians, special interest groups, and individuals) found success through concocted images and associations. The degree that the messaging misleads the audience varies, of course. If you Google "candy companies," you'll find sites with the word "old-fashioned" lodged in the name. Click and you'll find logos with horses and carts and 1800s villages, metaphors for freshness and purity. Yet the products contain artificial preservatives and colorings, old-fashioned as the PEZ dispenser. Is this a cute marketing slant, or a lie? The jury is out. But if you believe in heaven, stay on the safe side and play it straight.

The Brand Promise

Every time marketers create flash, they're setting expectations. If the flash experience is relaxing, the brand must relax the audience. If energizing, the brand must energize them, at least temporarily. The expectations are also about specific actions, or a brand promise. Billy Mays promised women miracle remedies for ordinary annoyances like forgetting to water their plants. TurboTax promises an easy solution to expensive tax processes. Lay's Potato Chips, with its tagline "So good, no one can eat just one," promises that the chip will be addictively delicious.

So, why isn't the audience let down? Two reasons. One, the audience is more certain about a brand after they purchase it than before. Second, the promise is assumptive or leading. "So good, no one can eat just one" assumes the audience will be aching for that second, third, and countless other chips . . . .

And they do.

The World's What?

In the movie *Elf*, we see the comic side of a brand not fulfilling its promise. Elf, played by Will Ferrell, moves to New York City after a lifetime living at the North Pole. He sees a coffee shop with the promise embedded in the tag: "The World's Best Coffee Sold Here." Elf goes racing into the coffee shop, shouting, "Congratulations you guys, you did it!" Everyone inside looks at him, incredulous. Did what? Made the world's best coffee!

Other people can determine how well a brand upholds its promise, especially in the rapid-fire universe of Internet conversations. An unhappy customer may post their opinions online, which may attract other unhappy customers, creating a negative viral effect.

Think of Nutrisystem's brand promise, which may seem to be about weight loss; it isn't. It's about delicious, guilt-free eating. The company's website and ads say:

> *Nutrisystem® D™ is nutritionally balanced and designed to help control hunger. Choose from over 100 delicious foods!*

The faces of the dieters are happy, not only because they lost weight but because they had such a pleasurable time doing it. The initial flash is supported by photos of sumptuous foods with names such as Double Chocolate Muffin, Maple Brown Sugar Oatmeal, and Egg Fritatta. But when I conducted a search for Nutrisystem on the web, I found a page from *www.consumer.com* (whose tagline is "Knowledge is Power") right under it. On it, I found this entry from Charlie of Chandler, Arizona (06/22/08):

> *I had used NutriSystem [sic] in the past a few years ago and the food was awful and made me very ill. I also could not order just what I wanted in the quantities I wanted so I stopped dealing with them. This time after seeing all the commercials I figured the food had to taste better and the service surely had to be improved. So reluctantly I ordered the vegetarian women's plan. I received the first order in April, 2008 and immediately began to identify the foods that were inedible . . . .*

FLASH FOR YOU: How can you determine your company's brand?
Ask your employees, freelancers, and consistent customers what they think of your business. Avoid focus groups—participants tend to engage in pack behavior and support the opinions of the most outspoken person in the group. Instead, e-mail a form to your target and provide a confidential place to deposit it. Or, set up a survey on your Intranet. You could always hire someone to talk with the employees in confidential interviews, as well. You'll find that a consensus of opinion will emerge. Then, with this information and essential qualities of your mission and vision, develop the campaign.

More about Brand: The "Them" in You

A brand does more than ignite a feeling in the audience: it establishes a relationship that will motivate and penetrate the entire campaign. Generally, brands fall into a number of categories. They can overlap, particularly if the campaign contains many facets. But here are the most common ones:

ASPIRATIONAL BRANDS

The flash sets off a sense of longing, desire, and possibly shame, tapping what the audience hopes—or aspires—to be. One of the most obvious examples is in the world of beauty and fitness. Women are easy targets because of their poor self-esteem. In fact, in a press release posted on its website, Dove tells us that just 12 percent of women are very satisfied with their physical attractiveness and only 2 percent describe themselves as beautiful.

Let's go back to Nutrisystem for a minute. Go on their website and you immediately see the image of Sarah who, they tell us, lost sixty pounds. And, in true testimonial form, we see Slender Sarah with a Fatter Sarah squeezed into a "before" type of photograph.

This is a typical strategy, which endures because it works. In his book *Influence: The Psychology of Persuasion* Robert Cialdini describes this as "The Contrast Principle":

> *Simply put, if the second item is fairly different from the first, we will tend to see it as more different than it actually is. So, if you lift a light object first and then lift a heavy object, we will estimate the second object to be heavier than if we had lifted it without first trying the light one.*

Another example is Maybelline. Founded in 1915, the company had this nondescript and nonaspirational tag: "The first modern eye cosmetic for everyday use." Now, their tag reads: "Maybe she's born with it, maybe it's Maybelline." Yes, we aspire to be Maybelline-like and that sells the product.

Yet, in spite of their success (an $80 billion industry if you include diet, cosmetics, and cosmetic surgery) women are pushing back. According to the Dove survey I quoted a minute ago,

68 percent of women strongly agree that the media set an unrealistic standard of beauty

75 percent wish the media did a better job in portraying the diversity of women's physical attractiveness, including size and shape, across all ages

In response, Dove (through its agency Ogilvy Mather) launched a different type of aspirational marketing campaign, in which you see women who actually *have* flesh posing in underwear. Here's what else Dove says on parent company Unilever's website: "Over the last few years, Dove has focused on delivering products that inspire women to enjoy their own beauty and individuality . . . ." The site claims that Dove can help you "bring out your real inner beauty."

In other words, the Dove campaign targets women who *aspire* to accept themselves. (If nothing else, the campaign generated buzz, and plenty of it. In the subway stations of large cities you see posters of women with decidedly un-tiny figures in their underwear and the tagline "Real Women Have Real Curves.")

This brings up another aspect of aspirational marketing: it tends to be negative. For Nutrisystem to sell its diet plan, the audience must think they're overweight—or why lose weight? For Maybelline to sell its beauty products, women must feel that they don't measure up. But the negative aspect of aspirational branding can be exhausting at times; Dove was one of the first to try a more positive approach.

Like so many companies, large and small, Dove also weaves "cause marketing" into its campaign. This means the company elevates its brand to a do-good, feel-good level, taking on one cause or another.

Dove's cause is the "Campaign for Real Beauty," and a part of it is the Dove Self Esteem Fund (DSEF). The object, says the website, is to "demonstrate our commitment to the brand's mission 'to make more women feel beautiful everyday.'" What they continue to say is, "The DSEF aims to educate and inspire young girls . . . which ultimately protects and nurtures their body-related self-esteem."

The next question is whether the campaign will help increase Dove sales. According to one blog comment on *www.adjab.com*, the company first launched its campaign in Europe, where Dove experienced a 700 percent increase in sales. This fact doesn't guarantee that the Dove campaign will be an overall success; as of this writing, no one can say.

RELATIONSHIP BRANDS

Relationship brands are probably the oldest of brand types: for centuries, stables, inns, even towns were named for their inhabitant or owners. The brand is an extension of that person or group of people, taking on their characteristics. The town where I live in West Virginia was once called Mecklenburg, named for the original founders, and the Mecklenburg Inn, originally built in the 1700s, is still a bar. Today the bar attracts locals around a brand built on history, and the residents own it. The bar, like the name, is theirs.

Apple's recent marketing campaigns, as we discussed in the previous chapter, focus considerably less on the value of Mac products and more on the personality of Steve Jobs and Bill Gates. For them, winning customers means winning friends—friends who have developed a *relationship* with the company and its products.

Insurance businesses know that creating a flash response based on familiarity and trust is critical in a difficult economy. Progressive's nameless girl-in-white exudes gleeful enthusiasm at the money the brand saves customers. State Farm's spokesman, Dennis Haysbert, reassures the audience in a deep, level voice. GEICO has a lineup of faces from the comical (the caveman), targeting a college demographic, to the sublime (Little Richard and Burt Bacharach) targeting boomers. And Nationwide replaced its humorous "Life comes at you fast . . ." campaign for one in which employees introduce themselves to the audience.

ONE MORE CASE STUDY

Massachusetts-based Jordan's Furniture has mastered relationship-based branding. They're all about a flash experience of happiness, humor, fun. The company's spokespersons are the former owners, Barry and Eliot (Warren Buffett owns it now), who inherited the family business. Their ads create an uplifting, happy flash experience for their audience based on their perennially relaxed and good-humored presence. Gradually, the brothers have built on that brand, promising more than a happy relationship; they promise a good time. The company hasn't reneged on the promise: the store now hosts a Broadband IMAX 3D Theatre; a 120,000-square-foot showroom with a Mardi Gras/Bourbon Street theme; and ongoing events.

FLASH FOR YOU: Grassroots relationship

If you are marketing a grassroots campaign, or own a small retail business, the relationship brand at one level or another is inescapable. Think about large corporations whose brands you purchase. Hewlett-Packard. Nintendo. Coca-Cola. When you think of these products, you think of brand qualities, taglines, or other factors that trigger flash. Now, think of your local dry cleaner, neighborhood pub, or preschool. Your relationship with these places may hinge on your experience with the owner. Even if you're a behind-the-scenes person, your personality will count.

ATTITUDE BRANDS

Marketers recognize the importance of the flash response and orient their efforts toward achieving it. But they're also generating an emotional response; mostly they want the audience to consciously recognize core points about their products: the price, the origin, and special features, to name a few.

Not so with attitude brand. That moment of flash, whether triggering feelings of sexiness, daring, hunger, or other strong emotions, cancels out any specific attributes of the brand. There are countless examples in the marketing universe. Take Calvin Klein. His products—from men's underwear to women's perfume—are about *attitude*, the *flash*, of Calvin Klein.

Martha Stewart's? Look at any magazine cover, any advertisement, any page of her website and you'll see her face dozens of times. As for Calvin? Go on his website: no Calvin. Look at his products: no Calvin. Instead, his ads, whether on New York City billboards or Calvin's website, reveal near-naked underwear models. Speaking of the website—when you go to the CK site (actually, Phillips–Van Heusen Corporation bought the company in 2002), you see a model on a runway with dangerously high spike heels and the expression of a heroin addict who just had a fix. And you see lots of images. No descriptions, promises, taglines, or testimonials. Calvin is about flash. The flash of sex, defiance, sex, intensity, sex, and attitude. Sexual attitude.

Attitude brand is easy for small online and neighborhood businesses to achieve. The flash comes from the most rudimentary efforts: the name, a sign on the door, the look of the building.

One example is The Blue Moon Café in Shepherdstown, West Virginia. The owners are baby boomers who maintain their hippie attitude. Their Gen Y employees are tattooed and pierced and politically off the edge—hovering somewhere near anarchy. As for the café, it has overgrown plants wedged into pots around the window, tables overlooking steady waterfalls from the town's run, and a distinctly un-plastic décor. The food is an aside: basic burgers with plenty of vegetarian options that are easy enough to prepare at home. The Blue Moon is a gathering place of like-minded people, and not a whole lot more matters.

NO-BRAND BRANDS

The no-brand brand or discount branding proves that even plainness, near-invisibility, can generate flash. The no-brand brand evokes a feeling that's all about accessibility, availability, with an instant brand promise of being affordable . . . a good deal. It stands out from the glitz and personality of competitive businesses. For some audiences, the flash may be one of relief.

One example is the Asian buffet phenomenon that has sprouted up around the country: buildings plain and unadorned, sign simply saying, "Chinese Buffet and Sushi Bar." Inside are lots of booths and aisles of foods; no logos, no taglines, no reminders of why you're there. The brand promise is clear: the place is all about food, limitless food, with no ornaments, cumbersome menus, or other distractions.

"Generic" products are another example. The flash inspired by their plain-wrapped packaging is potent and real. Plenty of chains have leveraged the power of the no-brand brand, such as the Dollar Store with its minimalistic interior and no-nonsense name. Even WalMart Stores, which obviously does an enormous amount of marketing, has historically had a no-brand brand with, for example, a no-nonsense interior. More recently, the chain has been trying to win a more upscale clientele and has added the tagline "Live Better. Save Money." as well as vibrant colors on its marketing messages.

WORD BRANDS

We've already discussed how neuromarketing can indicate which part of the brain is triggered by marketing messages. However, marketers are constantly fighting against the danger that the audience will forget the message or be more compelled by a sexier one. So while the short-term goal is to trigger a flash response, the marketer's ultimate, long-term goal is to create "flash memory" where the brand becomes internalized—part of the audience's independent, subjective experience.

Starbucks achieved this by entering the audience's internal vocabulary. "Coffee" can refer to anything: Peet's, Maxwell House, or a no-name cup from the local diner. But "Grande Latte Soy" is specifically Starbucks. Every time someone thinks it, craves it, or mentions it, they're automatically flashing on Starbucks.

Plenty of marketers try to own words—they trademark them, create acronyms from them, and repeat them in everything from giveaways to websites. But they're just owning words. Starbucks owns the entire vocabulary.

For example, Starbucks calls a small cup of coffee a *tall* cup, a light roast *mild*, and a dark roast *traditional*. For the sizes, they have *short* (which is actually not an option unless you want an espresso). That's a *short*, not an *extra small*. Then they have *small*, which they call *tall*. What follows next is a *grande*, which is Italian. But why drop English? Why not, for example, go from tall to taller? What follows *grande* is called *vente*. Vente?

Other advantages evolve from a word brand. Whenever a customer uses it with another person, they're providing word-of-mouth marketing value, also called carryover flash. They don't have to proclaim the virtues of Starbucks, or even discuss it. They simply need to say that they're getting "a Starbucks" or a "Skinny Cinnamon Dolce Latte" or any other Starbucks term.

If the customer tells a friend "I'm dying for a Cinnamon Dolce Latte," the friend has an empathetic response, sharing the excitement, pleasure, or longing. Should the customer be drinking the beverage at the time, the friend also experiences the smell and, quite possibly, the sound of the customer's satisfied drinking.

Marketers claim language in numerous ways. Here are a few of them:

Catchy-sounding

McDonald's can put its trademark "Mc" in front of virtually any food group or menu item, such as McNuggets, and immediately get the flash response cultivated by the company over the years. Just as significant, the prefix is catchy, giving musicality that's bouncy and upbeat, deepening the audience's experience of the word.

Usable

Starbucks' language works because you see it in writing, speak it, and *use* it every time you order. They're more than buzz words or abstract concepts: they're memorable because they're highly utilitarian. The more the customer uses these words, the more embedded they become in their internal vocabulary, and the more other people hear them.

Ever-present

Marketers include these words in everything: marketing material and press releases, sure, but also manuals, employees' sales scripts, and other internal documents. While external audiences are obvious targets for marketing campaigns, internal audiences are significant, too. They're often the ones who reinforce the brand promise, and therefore their activities, whether in front of customers or behind-the-scenes, must be consistent with the brand.

Brand Extension

Brand extension is a way of stretching that moment of flash as far as it can possibly go. So, Ralph Lauren moved from Polo clothes to Polo towels. Fighter George Foreman leveraged his name as a fighting champ (and gentleman) to promote his grill: manly, likable, and trustworthy. Arm & Hammer, maker of baking soda, reliable, safe, and old-fashioned, now sells laundry products. Other attempts at brand extension are less plausible. For example, Play-Doh has developed its own line of perfume, and Harley-Davidson created cake-decorating kits. Smaller businesses create brand extension when launching a new product. Perhaps the most ingenious marketing strategy occurs when the brand is actually the product, and the product a vessel for the brand. One example is a Boston-based store, Johnny Cupcakes, which was founded by Johnny Earle, a hard-metal rocker in his twenties. The store itself creates flash: the name, Johnny Cupcakes, and the clean, sparse exterior, immediately create a flash that is comforting and joyful, rooted in the visitor's earliest experience of the birthday parties of childhood.

Yet (and this is the weird bit) Johnny Cupcakes doesn't carry cupcakes. Initially, the store sold T-shirts, then added underwear and necklaces. The flash—and the expectation that it brings—isn't met by the reality. This can be intriguing, if not riveting, to some

audiences and annoying to others. But, it will pique the audien,
curiosity and create buzz.

The products aren't extraordinary, but they *do* have the Johnny
Cupcake design, defiant and stark, with the logo—a cupcake with
crossbones beneath. And that is primarily what the store sells: the
Johnny Cupcakes brand.

FLASH FOR YOU: Multibrands and why they're bad

Can my company have several brands, since we offer a variety of products
and services? Having several brands may seem logical, but you can't. You can
have a line of products and attract different demographics to each, but you
can't have separate brands. Think about McDonald's. It caters to kids—at
one time McDonald's distributed more toys to kids than any other company in
the United States. And the restaurants have the burgers, shakes, and fries for
guys with hungry bellies and thin wallets. McDonald's also realizes that not
everyone wants to eat grease or junk. So, the company added a salad bar. But,
can you call McDonald's a health-food restaurant? Not by a long shot. It's a
fast-food restaurant, quick and without frills.

CHAPTER 2:

Flash! Review

Core characteristics of your brand distinguish you from others in your field. They are authentic to your brand and important to every aspect of your marketing campaign. The flash experience that you generate through messaging should be a direct extension of these characteristics

You should reflect your brand in all your messaging, including:

- **Language**—from an ad to a customer service letter
- **Design**—from marketing material to the website policy page
- **Physical location**—including lobby, signs, and the building's interior
- **Online presence**—such as blogs, webpages, and videos posted on YouTube
- **Employees' style** of customer service

Your messaging can inspire a flash experience of happiness, security, and so on. That flash, and your ability to sustain it, eclipses all other aspects of your marketing efforts.

The audience responds to messaging that reflects their thoughts, taps their experience and their outlooks.

Your brand promise may be unspoken (a price tag indicating quality) or overt (So good, no one can eat just one), but your brand must fulfill that promise consistently.

You can orient your brand in numerous ways: aspirational, relationship, attitude, no-brand, branded language, or a combination of these.

3. The Big "D" of Demographics

Flash is the audience's preconscious response to messaging. But the sound, smells, words, and images that trigger the flash highly depend on the makeup of the audience. Without targeting a clear demographic, marketers throw messages into a vacuum. In fact, this is probably most small business owners' biggest mistake: they have great names, concepts, logos, and websites, but no clear idea about which audience will receive them.

This task has become more complex and problematic for marketers for several reasons:

1. The Internet, the primary marketing force, reaches multiple, and often unpredictable, demographics.
2. Age and gender roles have become blurred to the point where baby boomers are working well into old age and housewives are now house-husbands.
3. A barrage of marketing messages compete for the audience's attention every day.

Of course, marketers do zero in on distinct demographics. One example is Bawls G33K B33R, which certainly isn't targeting elderly women. Their demographic is young male geeks and gamers. The name "G33K B33R" contains a code that this demographic will immediately notice. This taps into feelings of exclusivity (it's a code they get) and ownership (the brand, the bottle is about them). In case you're not one of them, "G33K B33R" means "Geek Beer": the "3's" are computer geek language for "E's."

Now, let's look at some general attributes of the typical audience.

Flash for Everyone

It's more critical now than at any point in history to recognize the importance of flash in a marketing campaign. Today's audience members are impatient and less likely to mull over their feelings, cull though the possible repercussions of their decisions, analyze, or judge whether their first impressions should be lasting ones. The following are some of the causes of this behavior.

COMMUNICATIONS VENUES

Most consumers, especially the much-coveted Generation Ys or millennium children, are using venues that require speed, clarity, and energy. Texts, Twitter, and Facebook focus on the number of *characters*, not words. YouTube alleviates the need for words altogether. And websites, while managing to convey whole thoughts, still uses clipped language mixed with sound and videos to report news. These venues shape the way your audience receives information . . . and it's fast.

DISTRACTION LEVEL

According to Maggie Jackson, *Boston Globe* columnist and author of the book *Distracted*, we live in a state of constant distraction. We talk on cell phones, tap BlackBerries, and listen to iPods, while doing other things. At home the television blares incessantly—even when no one's watching. Distraction is more than a state of mind; it's a state of life. At work, we switch tasks every three minutes. On the road, 40 percent of young drivers text-message, and 60 percent of all Americans eat while driving. With all that divided attention, it's hard to fully focus on any one thing.

MARKETING AND ADVERTISING

If you've tried advertising to get word out about your brand or tried to convince someone to advertise on your website or other venue, you know times are tough. According to Malcolm Gladwell in *The Tipping Point: How Little Things Can Make a Big Difference*, "There is a growing sense of disaffection in the marketing world with the standard set of ideas and solutions that people are being presented with. I think actually the marketing community is approaching a crisis: There are just too many messages competing for too little attention."

In essence, when marketing anything—your service, product, idea, political position, or even your position on social issues—you're competing with thousands of other messages and an audience who doesn't pay attention. Flash isn't just the best way to reach your audience. It's all you've got.

And What Else? More Demographic Considerations

Knowing the demographic is important—but marketers also consider the following questions.

WHO IS THE BUYER?

The buyer may not be the one using the product. For example, adult children may choose everything from retirement homes to clothing for elderly parents. Wives frequently shop for their husbands and children. In the business world, administrative people often determine which supplies make it into the workplace.

But often the buyer may not be the person who's ultimately paying. For example, in senior living facilities the buyer may actually be the resident, while the child or even grandchild is the decision-maker. The elder care referral service "A Place for Mom" recognizes this fact. The name ignites a flash of calm, in a folksy sort of way, geared to alleviate the anxiety and guilt adult children typically feel when moving parents from their home.

Compare this to the Armed Forces Retirement Home, whose likely buyer is the seniors themselves. The tagline is "The Premier Retirement Community for America's Veterans." The message is that this is no place for the aged: the positioning is all about exclusivity, elegance, style. More significant, though, is the initial flash that occurs in that one-fiftieth of a second when the eye meets the retirement community's website. The words: "Flash Forward." The images: Seniors engaged in activities—gardening, playing cards. Energy and motion.

WHO INFLUENCES THE BUYING DECISION?

The pharmaceutical industry promotes its brands to health-care providers as well as the patient who's taking them. Manufacturers of educational products give schools free samples, discounts, and support should they use their brand. In both cases, the companies give the professionals free samples to pass on to others. This creates an interesting dynamic: since the trusted professional is giving the product, the product must be trustworthy, too. This is the marketing concept of carryover flash. More on that topic is coming up soon.

In a twist on the theme, marketers of cereal and other products for children send messaging through influencers (such as superheroes or pop stars) to kids, who associate the product with these heroes (if Buzz Lightyear uses it, it *must* be good). The message is ultimately positioned so the kids repeat the right information to their parents, by saying, for example, that the cereal has niacin and vitamin C.

WHAT MEDIUM DOES THE AUDIENCE CHOOSE WHEN RECEIVING INFORMATION?

Citizens in some rural communities still rely on television and mail and ignore the Internet altogether. Others, particularly urban youths, rely on Twitter and Facebook, to the exclusion of e-mail.

Other differences can be related to age: about 65 percent of baby boomers still read newspapers, while Generation Ys rely on the Internet. Then there's the saturation problem: Virtually every public space is occupied with a marketing message. Recently, for example, I was in the women's room of a hotel in Washington, D.C. As I went to wash my hands, an ad for FloMax starting running above the sink. The company Half.com put its logo on urinal screens.

This search for new venues landed some marketers on airplanes, the perfect marketing venue. Passengers have few distractions and nowhere else to go, making them a captive audience. Brands market in in-flight magazines, advertisements on tray tables, ticket jackets, cocktail napkins—even airsickness bags. They also advertise on tickers: the graphics are slowing down the time it takes travelers to print their tickets at the airport.

Demographics Down-Sizing

Very often, the narrower the demographic, the better the result. Donna Maria Coles Johnson is one example. A former corporate attorney, she started a business providing network opportunities and advice to stay-at-home women with soap-making businesses. A small demographic, yes, but a highly targeted one. She launched a website at which consumers could purchase products online as well as a radio show and a series of conferences. These numbered about 100 at first but quickly climbed to 700, a big number in the soap-making universe. The buzz about her spread, and she secured a profitable enterprise, which has expanded in scope significantly to encompass other beauty products as well.

Demographics: The Big Five

Marketers cluster their audience into five categories, more or less. These groupings are not siloed. For example, adolescent boys and their thirty-something fathers are often gamers, a group that cuts across the generational line. Further, the buyer of the games may be the father, although the purchases may be for the son. That said, the following are the main demographic factors.

THE AGE FACTOR

Most old men aren't remotely interested in Lego blocks, and most thirty-something women with toddlers are. Baby boomers aren't too concerned with birth control pills or, for that matter, training bras. More to the point, most boomers are less concerned with daring activities and intense sexuality; marketing messages intending to ignite flash using these strategies will only make this audience nostalgic or tired.

This is evident in the Viagra ads where we see boomers, about to have sex, talking and laughing as they stroll along the road on a nice day. The flash is one of control, evenness. Compare that ad to those for KY Jelly, ads that nicely trigger humor, excitement, and speed, with hilarious images of trapeze artists, swing dancers, and opera singers hitting high notes as metaphors *not* for orgasms, but for *better* orgasms.

Advertising Age writer Kenneth Gronbach, among others, breaks age demographics into key segments: the GI Generation, the Silent Generation, the Baby Boomers, Generation X, and Generation Y.

Their profiles look like this:

THE GI GENERATION

This generation is at least eighty-four years old, around 5 million strong. They're called the GI generation for their role in World War II, which was one of their two great contributions. (The other was parenting the most outrageous generation, the baby boomers.) Marketers generally target them for assisted living centers, funeral parlors, health-care options, and so forth, sticking to traditional media.

According to Gronbach, "This generation sleeps fitfully and often leaves the TV on during the night so they can have some company each time they wake up." It's important to remember that they grew up in an age of communications dignity. Grammar was absolutely correct and people read entire messages. Cute puns, grammar mistakes, overly relaxed language, and spicy content will engender the wrong flash experience from them. On the other hand, they're more forgiving and willing to get through an entire message before casting a final judgment.

THE SILENT GENERATION

Whoever dubbed them the "silent" generation hasn't met my parents or their friends. They were born between 1925 and 1944 and were, according to Gronbach, the smallest generation in 100 years, with 17 million still around. Apparently, they're not at their peak in terms of spending but are still willing to drop a dime for a good meal out or whatever it takes to keep them healthy and fit.

The study also tells us: "Pharmaceutical and insurance advertising are identified as the top categories where the 62-year-old and over market is most engaged. It also identifies additional categories such as package goods, travel, and entertainment, which includes movies, television shows and games as viable categories for marketing to this demographic segment."

Don't make the mistake of believing they're Internet-phobic; they're not. In fact, according to a study conducted by Focalyst and Dynamic Logic, each one is on the Internet for an average of forty-four minutes per day. While online, nearly 60 percent use search engines. In terms of flash, excitement is good, but be careful on the edginess. Like the GI Generation, they expect to be treated as customers before the purchase, meaning approaching them with respect and a certain amount of formality.

THE BABY BOOMERS

Look around and it's hard to believe they're the ones who ran nearly naked at Woodstock. But they are still a force and will be well past their collective deaths, I'm sure. There are 75 million around, born between 1945 and 1964. At one point not too long ago, they were hefty spenders, though the 2008–09 recession changed that for many of them.

The boomers save rather than spend, seeing how the realities (and restrictions) of retirement are increasingly real. They're still believers in conventional media—they could be the last holdouts for hardcopy newspapers. As we mentioned when discussing retirement homes (or other products for the elderly), boomers are often the target for such products and services. They're usually the ones caring for their GI Generation and Silent Generation parents or other relations, so marketers factor them into their elder-care marketing equation. Finally, according to LiveScience.com, boomers are basically an unhappy lot compared to other generations—a helpful fact if you're marketing Xanax.

GENERATION X

Born between 1965 and 1984, they're a small group—about 65 million—which, says Gronbach, "has dealt a death blow to many consumer-product manufacturers who are caught flat-footed and uninformed." In other words, there aren't enough of them to shape the direction of the marketing universe.

Still, they're products of the Internet age, witnessing its merger into the international bloodstream. They were the ones who invented Webzines and advocated for paperless books. They love excitement and newness, and are willing to try the latest thing. Remember: they, and a handful of older baby boomer parents, were the ones to play Mozart to their fetuses, thinking they'd come out smarter. Speed, immediacy, is their thing.

GENERATION Y

Born around 1985, they're the hot items in today's marketing universe. Here's why: Unlike the other demographics, they're still unwed in the product world. In other words, their tastes haven't solidified; they don't have that much coveted brand loyalty. The flash effect matters most with them; get the right response and you may have them for life.

The Yers, says Gronbach, consume at 500 percent times the rate of the baby boomers—which, if you've met my son, you know is absolutely true. Cyberspace is as familiar to them as the real world, only more desirable. This can make them hard to reach. People tend to float through the cyberworld, slipping around the never-ending tidal wave of information. They're impressive multitaskers, too, to the point of being culturally ADHD. Other news: They care about the values of those they purchase from; they're human rights- and ecology-minded.

Reaching Gen Y

Gen Y may be the newest (and youngest) thing to hit the marketing scene, but they're also among the most powerful. Ann Loehr, a Gen Y expert and author of *A Manager's Guide to Coaching: Simple and Effective Ways to Get the Best Out of Your Employees*, says the Obama campaign presents a perfect example of how to reach the Gen Yers. Says Loehr:

> The Facebook co-founder Chris Hughes directed Obama's new-media campaign. Hughes helped launch My.BarackObama.com, a digital staging ground for volunteer opportunities, phone bank requests and other events.

Many companies are using social media, yet few to the degree that Obama did. It's not enough to post your profile on Facebook, Twitter, or MySpace. You need to engage in it by posting events, writing on walls, creating groups and more, on a regular basis. At one point Obama had 1,899,998 Facebook fans (more than three times McCain's fans); 83,347 Twitter followers (versus McCain's 2,216 followers); and 20,636 MySpace friends (McCain had none).

Loehr also says that peer pressure plays a role in winning Gen Yers. She reasons that if a Gen Y sees that 65 percent of her friends like your company, product, or even your marketing campaign, they'll be inspired to give you a chance.

His 'n' Her: The Gender Divide

Although men and women have more in common in terms of lifestyle than they did a few decades ago, marketing to the genders remains radically different. One example is men's deodorant, which contains names such as "Cyclone," triggering flash feelings of power and danger. Women get softer, more soothing names such as "Orchard Blossom" and "Powder Fresh."

The distinction is consistent across many gender-targeted campaigns. Gold's Gym, for example, has a primary appeal to men, with its logo of a silhouetted old-time weightlifter, although increasing numbers of women are joining. The tagline is "Know Your Own Strength," and the colors on the website homepage are primarily blacks, grays, and blues.

Curves, which exclusively targets women, has the tagline "Your Curves will amaze you . . ." with web colors of pastel pinks and purples, much like those on boxes of sanitary products.

The flash experience is about acceptance, reassurance, and happiness.

The two fitness centers demonstrate a typical difference in how marketers approach men and women. Gold's Gym is all about strength and power, while Curves is about appearance. Gold's tells its audience to know themselves; Curves tells women, albeit indirectly, that by going to the gym they'll look better for others.

Chicken or Egg?

Does marketing drive our culture or the other way around? The issue weighs more heavily when marketers target specific gender and age and ethnic groups. Are marketers responsible for shaping the culture and well-being of their demographic? If companies realize their products create destructive behaviors in specific groups, should they target them anyway, knowing their profits will go up? We'll return to these critical questions as we go on.

Overall, marketers focus more on women than men for many reasons. One is that there are more of them; according to the U.S. Bureau of the Census, as of October 1, 2007, there were 153.6 million females in the United States and only 149.4 million males. The online universe, which many have considered a male's domain, is visited more frequently by women, as well. In fact, in the next few years 72.1 percent of females versus 69.3 percent of males will be going online.

As I mentioned earlier, numerous sources indicate that women possess over 80 percent of the spending power in the United States. And that doesn't mean only soccer outfits for the kids or diapers for the babies. It means real estate, automobiles, and, increasingly, technology. An increasing number of women are business owners, as well. Some estimates have it that more than half of all small business owners are women—many of these businesses grassroots operations with offices within the house.

Women also live an average of ten years longer than men, which means they get ten extra years to vote, volunteer, and influence their communities on everything from ethical issues to brand purchases. And speaking of community, women head up the majority of single-parent households, which means they have overwhelming responsibility for raising the next generation.

As well as being coveted, women are pursued. Many of those roughly 7,000 messages we receive a day target the female demographic; 400 to 600 alone are about looks. They infiltrate virtually every aspect of a woman's life.

Then, look at medical reports, newspaper articles, and television broadcasts with a huge number of marketing messages per story. Blogs, chatrooms, and Facebook profiles nearly ooze marketing influences. They're on the billboards at the side of the road, labels on everything from shampoo to laxatives, medical alerts from the doctor, and signs in store windows. Turn on the radio— they're there. Go to the movies—there again, neatly embedded in the plot.

Naturally, ventures specifically targeting women are rising at a furious rate. Yahoo! recently launched "Shine," a site focusing on twenty-five- to fifty-four-year-old women. Other online marketers targeting the female demographic include Glam Media, iVillage.com from NBC Universal, AOL Living, and Everyday Health. And don't forget *www.Wowowow.com*, a site targeting upscale women over forty brought to you by gossip columnist Liz Smith, television journalist Leslie Stahl, and political pundit Peggy Noonan, among others. Last, though hardly least, there are countless marketing campaigns that target women, from Avon, which calls itself "the company for women," to agencies that devote whole workforces to determining how to reach this coveted group.

In the face of this tidal wave of marketing messages, women remain relationship-oriented. In decision-making at work, for example, they tend to seek consensus rather than make top-down decisions. Marketers recognize this and reach them through carry-over flash, finding influencers who engage them in online "conversations" about everything from raising kids to sexuality. The flash around women's issues may be edgy, energetic, and outrageous, but it also contains a more reassuring effect, especially as women move into family and motherhood.

FLASH FOR YOU: Is she right for me?

If you're thinking about targeting women, whether intensely or exclusively, then look at how your women-centric marketers position their information. Check out Shine, *www.Wowowow.com,* and the other sites I mentioned here. But also look at advertisers who target women when marketing everything from sanitary napkins to power suits for work. At this point, yours is not to question, but to observe. Then decide what works for your brand.

Mother Power

Every demographic is broken into subdemographics, as you know. One subset of the women's category is mothers; an important—perhaps the most important—demographic on the marketing landscape. The reason is clear: Mothers influence the buying decisions of their children directly, by the products they purchase, and indirectly, through the lifestyles they encourage. And children = a better shot at brand loyaltybecause once they like something, they may like it for life.

This is obvious to marketers from the Partnership for a Drug-Free America. On its website, the organization says: "The Partnership for a Drug-Free America is a nonprofit organization that unites parents, renowned scientists and communications professionals to help families raise healthy children." While men do have a presence on the site, the images are primarily of women, presumably mothers.

The nonprofit's website also contains a social network, Timetotalk.org, which taps directly into women's consensual, community orientation. In terms of flash, it's geared to sooth and engage: the visitor does *not* get an alarming or anxiety-provoking fla~~ ~~ith images of strung-out kids or horrid facts about the num~~ ~~eaths due to drug addiction. This one taps the nurturing side of the demographic: it's all about "conversation," "find out" helpful pointers, and smiling faces.

Given women's community orientation, marketers do well by reaching women indirectly. One Keller Fay study conducted for the BabyCenter, an online resource for new and expectant mothers, tells us that pregnant and new mothers get lots of product and brand information through good old-fashioned kitchen talk—in other words, word of mouth or carryover flash. In fact, they have over 109 word-of-mouth conversations each week—one-third more each day than anyone else.

The research group MindShare also tells us that reading and web and television viewing are the top ways mothers spend their "me time" and that:

- 56 percent of mothers spent "me time" in the late evening, while 18 percent took it in the early morning.
- Mothers with children under the age of two considered so-called word of mouth as the best "entertainment media," while others liked television, then e-mail.
- Nonworking mothers used e-mail the most, and part-time working mothers the least.

According to MindShare, part-time working moms reportedly felt the most stressed in their daily lives.

The Ethnic Majority Factor

Marketers are investing huge amounts of time and money into determining how specific ethnic groups respond to messages. Latinos, for example, are the largest immigrant group in the nation. So, when targeting this demographic, marketers shouldn't present a landscape full of gringos listening to Barry Manilow. Further, in a few decades, over 50 percent of the nation will consist of non-white consumers. This fact is already reshaping marketing's formerly white-centric approach.

Plenty of marketers target specific ethnic groups, sometimes for the right reasons, and sometimes for the wrong. One example is a report from the Campaign for Tobacco-Free Kids, which says:

> The tobacco industry has gone to great lengths to target the African-American community over the past 30 years. Through market research and aggressive advertising, the industry has success-fully penetrated this population. The industry's "investment" in the African-American community has had a destructive impact: African Americans suffer the greatest burden of tobacco-related mortality of any ethnic or racial group in the United States.

> Research shows that cigarette company advertising and other marketing efforts greatly influence tobacco use initiation among ado-lescent non-smokers and maintenance among those youths who have already become regular smokers. Eighty percent of all smokers start before the age of 18 and, not surprisingly, the vast majority of kids smoke the three most heavily advertised brands. One of these heav-ily advertised brands, Newport, is the cigarette brand leader among African-American youths in the United States. Eight out of every ten black, youth smokers smoke Newport cigarettes.

Most surprising is a quote from one R.J. Reynolds Tobacco Com-pany executive on the Campaign for Tobacco-Free Kids website: "We don't smoke that s _ _ _. We just sell it. We reserve the right to smoke for the young, the poor, the black and stupid."

Clearly, R.J. Reynolds will have to rethink its strategy and attitudes. The website *www.ethnicmajority.com* tells us, "The growth of Ethnic minorities in America has been phenomenal. Since 1980, the Asian American population has almost tripled, Hispanic American more than doubled, Native American increased 62 percent, and African American increased 31 percent, while the nonethnic population has remained almost the same. This trend is expected to continue. The latest estimates by the U.S. Census Bureau predict that the minority population will comprise fully half the U.S. population by the year 2050."

Any good marketer would be remiss to ignore the Latino population, for many reasons. Consider the brand loyalty factor. One remarkable aspect of this demographic is their youth. According to the U.S. Census of 2000, around 35 percent of Hispanics were under eighteen, and only 5.3 percent are sixty-five years old or above. The reason? Kenneth Gronbach of *Advertising Age* says that Latinos came to fill employment slots left empty by the small number of Generation Xers. Some may return home once the jobs market shrinks but others, many others, will stay.

According to the Bureau of the Census, here's what you can expect in terms of numbers:

- **2020:** about 52.7 million
- **2040:** about 80.2 million
- **2050:** about 96.5 million, or 24.5 percent of the U.S. population

Marketers know this demographic's brand loyalty is relatively unformed. As for spending, voting, and lobbying power, Latinos aren't at the top of the societal ladder—not yet, anyway—but do have power. In fact, they will soon be a major force, one of the biggest in the nation.

Reaching the Latino population is another matter. Marketers have had relatively little success online. According to the Pew Research Center, only 56 percent of Latinos go online from any location, and only 29 percent have a broadband connection at home.

When addressing any international or immigrant population, marketers must tread lightly—a fact many seem to forget. In the publication *Search Engine Watch*, Michael Bonfils explains the issue this way: "Every culture across the world is different. So if something works in one country, attempting to mirror it and expecting it to work in another country will certainly lead to failure."

He says the flashpoints for websites vary: "The French consider 'price points' as a key to decision making when searching for products online. The Germans look for 'quality' in their products as opposed to just price. Koreans look for 'technical complexities' as a key decision maker and the Japanese look for the sites' ability to gain their 'trust.'"

The level of detail in an international market is significant, though. One marketing firm created a website for a Middle Eastern university. On the homepage, they showed a group of laughing students walking through the campus and, in another, a mixed gender group swimming. The intention may have been to create a flash of fun for an international audience. But the campaign created an entirely different flash experience for the client whose culture and religion prohibited this type of interaction between genders.

FLASH FOR YOU: Cultural sensitivity

Will Sullivan has worked on international campaigns for the communications firm Fleishman-Hillard International for clients in places like Japan and Saudi Arabia. He offers this advice to marketers:

Be well versed in cultural issues. One size most definitely doesn't fit all in any culture—the interests and concerns vary depending on age, gender, income, and other factors.

Be aware of the subtle aspects of your campaign. You may have a mixed audience: some may have lived in the West and some may not have. So, be aware of the subtle references, jokes, and metaphors. Some may get it, some may not, and some might be offended.

Rely on visuals. Pictures, photographs, and Flash animation all speak a thousand words but, more to the point, a thousand languages.

Be alert to younger audiences. They're increasingly web savvy. They use it and talk to their friends about it. They are, in essence, purveyors of buzz.

Location, Location, Location

Location is playing a greater role in audience demographics. If a marketer in Boulder, Colorado, is positioning a ski lodge, she may need to create a flash experience of excitement, challenge, and fun to an audience in San Diego. Consumers must be convinced to hop on a plane and head over. But if targeting an audience in Denver, the marketer may need to create a flash experience of ease, pleasure, and accessibility so the audience will head her way and not to a nearby slope.

One of my clients, a federal agency, needed to reach a spectrum of Americans about health-related issues. You may not think this is a marketing matter, but it is. They needed to win over the population so they would use a new service that would more or less ensure their well-being in some circumstances.

The agency's core target group, though, lived in rural areas, places where suspicion of the government runs high. The moment they saw the federal logo on the message, they had a highly negative flash response. With the halo effect, they were less likely to accept or even read the message. And, they were more likely to seek legal counsel or have a friend or other advocate weigh in . . . *even though the issue was fundamentally not controversial.*

To offset the negative flash, the agency relied on "influencers": elected officials who would publicize the new program in the most upbeat terms, so the population would welcome it. When targeting a highly sophisticated urban audience, particularly in the greater D.C. area, the agency and its marketers could still rely on influencers, but their government status was less of a problem than in rural America.

As explained in Flash For You, marketers are of necessity finding new and instructive ways to address the nation's financial woes.

FLASH FOR YOU: Upscale in down times

You can position your offering as upscale even in bad times (think BMW, Starbucks, and Chubb Insurance). But show the benefit versus price no matter what. Recently, for example, Mercedes-Benz started focusing its marketing initiatives on safety.

Emphasize the lifestyle improvements of your brand. In hard economic times, people don't feel great. They want products and services that will soften the path through the financial spikes, ease their tensions, and return them to relative normality. Virtually any product, if it's good, can achieve this.

Shift or expand your campaign to target a different demographic, if necessary. Some boomers and most certainly their parents get hit pretty hard in economic downturns. So you need to determine how your brand will help them, in spite of their low cash flow. If it doesn't, reposition your pitch and, possibly, your brand to reach a target who will benefit more.

Take heart. Your brand is good. And your audience still needs products and services that are quality. So, step up your marketing campaign and keep the motion going! If nothing else, think of your marketing efforts as creating flash memory that will bring the audience your way later.

CHAPTER 3:

Flash! Review

The success of your marketing campaign is shaped by your demographic's relationship to marketing: the venues encourage brevity and speed; they're easily distracted; and they don't trust marketing.

Your buyer may be different from the person using your brand. Baby boomers may shop for their older parents, and Gen Xers may shop for their Gen Y kids. So, carefully determine who your buyers really are.

The optimal flash experience will vary from one demographic to another: While both are about a great sexual experience, KY Jelly is about excitement, while Viagra is about security and connection.

Specific visuals, sounds, or references may trigger a certain flash experience in one audience and a considerably different one in another. Cultural sensitivity, among other factors, is key.

Different demographics access messages through different vehicles: online, in print, through tweets, and YouTube videos.

Your brand may be new to some demographics and not to others—Gen Y will find almost anything that's technical to be familiar, but their baby boomer parents may be perplexed and amazed.

Many demographics cross traditional lines of gender, age, and interests. I know a boomer woman who likes to box, and plenty of children convince their parents to purchase toys, games, and other objects for them.

PART 2
THE RUSH OF FLASH

4. Name, Tag, and Attitude

Does flash indicate the first response an audience has to a marketing message? Yes . . . and no. Let's start with the true aspect: consumers have a flash experience when they first encounter a message. Try this little test to get a sense of the flash experience:

> *Spit in a cup then drink it. That's our soda!*

You probably had a strong feeling of revulsion, squeamishness, even queasiness. That's flash.

But marketers have trouble knowing when that first encounter will occur. When customers find a website through a search engine, for example, they could end up anywhere, not necessarily on the home-page. They may catch an ad in the middle or end or hear a pitch from a sales rep before knowing the name of the brand, its purpose, or tagline.

The halo effect may shape that flash experience. For example, read the line from the previous fictitious ad again:

> *Spit in a cup then drink it. That's our soda!*

Would you feel any differently and be eager to try the brand, if the line said:

Our soda is low-cal and healthy.

What you now get is a completely different kind of flash.

For most brands, though, the first and most important marketing element the audience will confront is the brand name. Let's look at what makes it so effective.

What's in a Name?

The names of businesses and their products reveal a great deal about the changing nature of marketing and the role of flash. Here are a few examples.

THE SWEETNESS OF CANDY BRANDS

Hershey's Chocolate was founded by Milton Hershey and his wife, Catherine, in 1894 in Lancaster, Pennsylvania. Hershey was one of the first to mass-produce chocolate, making a luxury item affordable to the public. Hershey's early candy had such names as LeRoi de Chocolate, Petit Bouquets, and Chocolate Croquettes. The flash point obviously came from the sound of the language: not salt-of-the-earth rural Pennsylvania but French, which triggers a flash experience of distinction, taste, and luxury. Hershey later repositioned the chocolates to reach a varied audience. According to the company history:

Some chocolate cigarettes and cigars, such as Vassar Gems and Smart Set Cigarettes, were purposely marketed to women as an alternative to the tobacco variety. Chocolate was also touted as a source of quick energy for athletes. The packaging for National Chocolate Tablets, which showed a bicyclist and baseball batsman, proclaimed that "wheelmen and ball-players will find them very beneficial."

Notice that the name "National Chocolate Tablets" triggers an altogether different flash: it's medicinal, straightforward, on the brink of patriotic. "Smart Set Cigarettes" creates a flash of stylishness, classiness, attractiveness.

An interesting footnote to the Hershey story is that Milton and Catherine Hershey were childless. So, they established The Milton Hershey School, an orphanage for boys. The couple left most of their fortune to the school, which now resides in Hershey, Pennsylvania, and is home and/or school to 2,000 low-income boys and girls. The school is the company's largest shareholder . . . and beneficiary of the chocolate fortune.

Another candy company, NECCO, based in New England, entered the candy scene in 1847, when Abe Lincoln was still a congressman and only twenty-nine states were in the Union. Originally, the company was known as the Chase Candy Company. Founder Oliver Chase invented the Peppermint Lozenge cutter, offering an alternative to hand-shaped candies. One of Chase's products was a sweet, round wafer, now known as the Necco wafer, which Union soldiers ate during the Civil War. In 1901, the Chase Candy Company merged with three others to become the New England Confectionary Company, or NECCO.

The name change is instructive on many levels. As we mentioned in the previous chapter, relationship branding (conscious or not) was a staple of marketing in the United States through the turn of the twentieth century. So, company names naturally reflected the owners. Brands that exist today include those of Eliphalet Remington, who developed the Remington gun in 1816 (and later the typewriter and razor) and Henry Reese, who created the peanut butter cup. (Reese was a disgruntled dairy farmer and former employee of Hershey. He opened his candy company a few miles down the road from the Hershey Chocolate Company. The two business owners were on amiable terms, and Hershey eventually bought out Reese for $23.5 million in 1963.)

While some entrepreneurs still name their businesses after themselves, industrialization and improvements in transportation changed the nature of business at the beginning of the twentieth century. The name "NECCO" reflected that change. Today, corporations, such as AT&T and Sprint Nextel Corp, have overtly corporate names. Does this diminish their flash? Not at all: the audience for their corporate messages is investors, regulators, and others who travel in that universe. Yet, when Sprint Nextel describes itself to consumers through marketing, they're "Sprint." The name has enormous flash: it triggers feelings of speed, energy, motion, and competitiveness.

An interesting footnote: Around 1866, Daniel Chase, Oliver's brother, created "Conversation Candies" with messages encoded on the wrapper. Some years after, they renamed the candies "Sweethearts," which were flat disks, later reshaped as hearts, imprinted with love messages. The conversation hearts originated right after-what was then called the War between the States and could have had a patriotic or war-related theme. But they went for sweethearts, instead.

In terms of flash, "Sweetheart" works perfectly. The word "sweet" has multiple meanings and associations, all positive: the flavor of sweetness, the temperament of "sweet people," and the pet name "sweet" as in "my sweet." The name encompasses the romantic aspect of sweethearts: the heart as a symbol of romantic love and the romantic term "sweetheart." Thus, the name activates our emotions, sense of taste, and curiosity.

The flash is immediate and real, as the candy fulfills the brand promise: it's tasty and romantic; love messages printed on pastel-colored candy. Even better, it's engaging and interactive: the audience reads the messages and shares them.

Today, NECCO invites the public to submit sayings, which now include such contemporary comments as "fax me."

Name That Brand

Finding a name for a new product, concept, or service can be difficult. Professional name-makers have numerous strategies, which all hinge on the personality of the brand. Following are some of the most essential qualities.

REFLECT YOUR BRAND

The Lost Dog reflects the coffee shop's brand: the furnishings are yard-sale specials and the customer base, while varied, has a high number of modern-day hippies.

BE MEMORABLE

It's always beneficial to tap the senses, giving the audience something to see, smell, or feel. The name "Johnny Cupcakes," which I mentioned earlier, taps smell, sight, taste, and a host of associations, more provocative because that's all Johnny Cupcakes is not. Be careful of names that are difficult to pronounce or spell: the audience won't remember them.

INVITE THE AUDIENCE INTO YOUR CLUB

Your name reflects the culture of your business: it speaks of attitude, promises a relationship, and provides evidence of the fit for a specific demographic. In a sense, it's like a club, inviting a like-minded audience to join.

FLASH WITH GENDER

Nowhere is the power of flash as obvious and discriminating as it is in names that specifically target men or women. Here are a few examples.

Energy drinks—guy style

The first energy drinks originated in Asia in the 1960s and migrated to the United States over the decades that followed. The drinks are marketed to high school and college age males but have picked up where traditional energy drinks (think Coca-Cola) have left off. The flash they engender is undoubtedly a mixture of audacity and brilliance.

1. **Full Throttle.** Manufactured by the Coca-Cola Company, "Full Throttle" is an excellent example of flash: it's encompassing, triggering the emotion of energy (driving a car, truck, or motorcycle at full throttle); the physical feeling of the vehicle beneath and around you; the excitement of fear and anxiety about going full throttle; and the undeniable sexiness of it all. Full Throttle puts the audience off-balance. There's something slightly illegal or dangerously inherent in its flash.
2. **Monster.** The flash from "Monster" is about defiance and power. To the right audience, however, it also triggers a sense of fun or play. This point is underscored by the logo of bright green claw marks just above the name, and the tagline: "Unleash the beast"

(rhymes have an element of surprise, which is one quality of humor). As well, the bottle features tongue-in-cheek marketing: "Tear into a can of the meanest energy supplement on the planet." The humor creates a sense of belonging to a special club whose members get the joke and enjoy it.

3. **Bawls and Bawls.** No one (including my thirteen-year-old, who is intrigued with the stuff) can deny that the name "Bawls" has a decidedly male meaning, creating a flash of surprise, humor, defiance, and energy that attracts specific male demographics. On its website, makers Hobarama LLC deny the association, saying: "Named for the caffeinated 'Bounce' it gives you, BAWLS gets its flavor and kick from the Amazonian Guarana berry, which contains a natural form of caffeine nearly three times stronger than that found in traditional sodas."

More interesting, though, is the root beer–flavored beverage called "Bawls: G33K B33R." As I mentioned earlier, "G33K B33R" means "Geek Beer": the "3's" are computer geek language for "E's." It still triggers the defiant, off-center flash that we discussed regarding Monster.

His/her deodorant

Compare the names of deodorant and you get yet another reason why John Gray named his book *Men Are from Mars, Women Are from Venus*. Marketers certainly treat the genders as if they were from separate universes. Start with the names of women's deodorants:

- Passion Flower
- Citrus Squeeze
- Kissed Peach
- Blue Flower

On the surface, these names refer to something in nature, flowers or fruits. But more significant, they tap numerous senses: smell, as flowers, peaches, and citrus are fragrant; feel, since all are soft; and relationship-based. You see this most clearly in "kissed" and "squeezed," but our associations with flowers are ultimately about gift giving. The flash is ultimately one of comfort, desirability to others, and passivity. The peach, the flowers, even the *blue* flower is about as gentle as it gets.

Now, compare that to the men's deodorants:

- Fresh Oxygen
- High Endurance
- Arctic Force
- Iron Man

These are sports-oriented, with words like "endurance" and "oxygen." They're about power, strength, tenacity. Arctic Force, High Endurance. Iron Man.

I probably don't have to tell you this, but both groups of products contain these ingredients:

- Active ingredient: aluminum zirconium tetrachlorohydrex glycine complex
- Other: water
- Cyclomethicone
- SD Alcohol 40
- Tripropylene glycol dimethicone

Same products, different names, different flash.

The Flash Promise

We discussed flash promises in the previous chapter. One way that marketers make compelling flash promises is through the brand's name. Sometimes the promise is obvious, other times not. Here are a few examples:

FREE CREDIT REPORT

When it comes to flash, the word "free" is brilliant. Enter Free Credit Report. The promise is clear: go online and get your credit report free. Actually, the name should be "$49.95-Each-Month-Credit-Report" since the company will continue to monitor the customer's credit *for a fee* after that first report rolls in.

This arrangement occurs thanks to another marvel of modern advertising: the membership list. Customers automatically receive their membership, which kicks in within seven days. The promise is there, but the reality isn't.

SAM'S CLUB

Sam's Club, (part of the WalMart family), similar to BJ's Wholesale Club and many others, makes a promise that is not about bargains, wholesale prices, or money-saving opportunity. It's about exclusivity. By joining one of these clubs for a nominal amount—usually under $100 a year—the audience can be part of a select group to receive prices *others do not get*. The irony is that this exclusive club lets everyone in. That aside, the flashpoint is not the word "wholesale," but "club."

UNIVERSITY OF PHOENIX

Overtly, the name University of Phoenix is about a university based in Phoenix: that's obvious. But the promise of the name is built around one word: "Phoenix." In case you have forgotten your mythology, the Phoenix is the bird that rises from its own ashes to begin life again. This promise is consistent with the University of Phoenix mission, as stated on its website:

If you've wondered how you can pursue a college education while working or raising a family, you're not alone. Many University of Phoenix students wondered the same thing, but more than 400,000 alumni are proof that it's possible.

We've empowered students from all walks of life to take control of their educational goals and earn a degree that works for them—personally and professionally.

Astroturfing

One phenomenon that's become increasingly common is astroturfing. That refers to political groups, advertisers, and PR firms posing as grassroots efforts around some issue. One example is "Rick Berman's Center for Consumer Freedom." The name sounds like a group of take-charge citizens . . . and is intended to sound that way. Actually, the organization is a front for the tobacco, restaurant, and alcoholic beverage industries.

WORD TWISTS

Puns or double entendres can spur the audience to spend more time on the name, and ride the flash moment a little longer. One example is Child's Play, a store in Bethesda, Maryland. The word "play" obviously ignites feelings of lightness, joy. But it has a twist: that finding a gift for a child is easy, or "child's play."

Another example is a toy store in Gloucester, Massachusetts, called "Fun Among Us." The name has a bouncy musicality, a quality of onomatopoeia, that resonates in a physical sense: we can *feel* the sound "Fun Among Us" compared to, say, "Fun Together."

Now What? The Wrong Name at the Wrong Time

To test the power of names as a marketing tool, see if you can guess the brands that were originally called:

- Free Disk Space
- The Mining Company
- Stag Party

Notice the difference between the original and the current choices:

- Free Disk Space: this awkward sound morphed into the cooler MySpace.
- The Mining Company. Not a coal company. It's About.com.
- Stag Party. A hunting club? Actually, it's *Playboy* magazine.

Frequently companies struggle with the name issue for reasons other than marketing clout, such as a scandal. For example, what feelings do the following brands trigger in you?

- Arthur Andersen
- John Edwards

Most likely, the flash you experienced from each of these brands was negative.

The Arthur Andersen accounting firm was devastated by its involvement with the collapse of Enron in 2001. While only a small group was associated with the scandal, because of the repeated negativity in the media over a relatively short time, even today the name Arthur Andersen generates a flash of suspicion, an insurmountably huge liability for an auditing firm. If the public were more contemplative, they might understand Arthur Andersen's underlying integrity.

Often, when a name shifts from being a selling point to a liability, a brand simply renames itself. Would you bank with a failing auto financier like GMAC? Rather than wrestle with the exhausting and unlikely task of changing public perception, GMAC morphed into Ally Bank. Other name changes include ValueJet, whose plane crashed in the Everglades and resurfaced as AirTran Airways; and Altria, once known as the cancer-causing cigarette producer Philip Morris. As a marketing choice it works—why not start again? But it is also misleading, robbing the audience of important information about the institution—and their choice to do business there. GMAC Chief Executive Al de Molina claimed the company's renamed business intends to "treat customers with total transparency." Huh?

On a more positive note, plenty of brands adopt new names because they have grown, shifted their product line, or because the names became outdated. Any brand with a name that includes "2.0," the word "buzz," or the term "social networking" is already outdated; these concepts are old, boring news.

In fact, the communications world spins into new universes so rapidly and unpredictably that any brand naming itself after the fad of the moment is foolish. A while back, we discussed the energy drink "Bawls G33K B33R." I mentioned that it creates an instant bond with so-called geeks. But the geek talk of replacing E's with 3's will be short-lived, and the name will have an early death.

FLASH FOR YOU: Name change?

Does your brand need a name change? The question is a strategic one. If your brand has been around for a while, and people know it, you have so-called brand equity, so think carefully before changing it. When people see it, they have a flash response you may have spent years cultivating. If you want to go in an entirely new direction, a change can help . . . but be aware that you need to reflect the feeling of that name in your marketing efforts.

Marketers use other strategies to reinvent themselves. Here are a few:

1. Change the name slightly. This is typical of smaller businesses that add new products, or firms that add partners. Changing the name slightly provides numerous benefits: from a flash perspective, it indicates growth to customers (something positive and exciting) yet maintains the brand recognition and, above all, is affordable.

2. Change the tagline. Most brands change their taglines regularly, anyway. Still, when a name is behind the times but the brand loyalty is worth saving, the tag can help. One example is Massachusetts Envelope Company. This family-run business started in the early part of the twentieth century. The name wore out its purpose, given that envelopes aren't exactly a hot commodity. But the family wanted to keep the name. So they added the tag "More than an envelope."

3. Change the name but create a PR opportunity by sending out press releases, notices, and online announcements. This creates

a flash of excitement and trust because the business appears to be growing and getting better, and the audience can share in that growth.

More about Names, Flash, and Function

Some brands deliberately make their name their address so people can immediately find them. One such brand is Amazon.com; another is SBTV.com, which stands for "Small Business Television." If you key in the name in a browser address bar, you'll head directly to the homepage, where you'll find the television with a news report and special features targeting the small business audience.

Names can generate a highly specific flash simply by being an expression of the "attitude" of the brand (see previous chapter). With many small businesses, home-based products, and bloggers, the name flows naturally. Here are some examples of blogs:

- Mighty Girl
- Book Square

The first belongs to author and editor Maggie Mason, whose blog you can find at *www.Mightygirl.com*. Maggie wrote a book for bloggers, which is well worth noting for the name alone: *No One Cares What You Had for Lunch: 100 Ideas for Your Blog*. Among Maggie's list of favorite blogs:

- Defective Yeti
- Dollarshort
- Dooce
- Finslippy
- Fussy

- Kottke
- Kung Fu Grippe
- Mimi Smartypants
- Not Martha
- Que Sera Sera
- Whole Lotta Nothing
- Whoopee

"Book Square," the blog of Kassia Krozser, focuses on the publications universe. Her site links to blogs with names such as "Smart Bitches Who Love Trashy Novels" and "Lusty Lady," but most are less edgy, with a flash that's distinctly different from those on Maggie's list:

- A Writer's Life
- Medialoper
- Reading Under The Covers
- RomanceWiki
- Romancing The Blog
- Shaken & Stirred
- The Happy Booker
- The Vintage Reader
- The Writers Life

Taglines

Taglines are critical to the marketing process because they're "sticky." They're longer than names, but not as long as, say, ad copy, so they're memorable and more likely to deepen the flash experience.

But what makes a tagline great? Why do they become part of our communications outside of the marketing realm? The answers tell us an incredible amount about how marketing campaigns motivate audiences to take action. If you had to boil it down, you would say this: truly compelling taglines contain tension that throws the audience off-kilter. Don't think that tension is necessarily bad. Anxiety or concern throws us out of balance, but quite possibly because we don't want to miss a sale. Humor works because of the element of surprise, the jolt you get from the unexpected.

Let's identify the tension in some taglines that have made it into the marketing hall of fame. Before we do, though, why not jot down a few of the taglines you remember from childhood. If you have a tagline for your own brand, whether a product, a campaign, or a business, write that down, too.

Perdue's tagline was, "It takes a tough man to make a tender chicken." The juxtaposition of "tough man" and "tender chicken" create the tension. The audience must slow down and reconsider the connection, deepening their engagement. You may also remember that the founder, Frank Perdue, looked like a chicken.

Peter Paul Mounds Bar used the tagline, "Sometime you feel like a nut, sometimes you don't." The line premiered in 1953 and enjoyed a pretty long run. The tension comes from the play on "feel" and "nut." "Feel" can mean how you feel about yourself or a yearning, while "nut" is the literal nut or a crazy person. The connotation with "nut," though, is positive (a "nutty" fun-loving person), and the flash is uplifting.

The classic *Star Trek* line, "To boldly go where no man has gone before." contains a split infinitive, an error that English teachers shunned for years. That tension, and the strength of the adverb "boldly," make the tagline work. The grammatically correct version, "To go boldly . . ." just doesn't have the same ring.

In 1956 Timex launched the tag, "It takes a licking and keeps on ticking." It touches on the physical (licking meaning "beating") and the metaphorical and has a nice, sticky rhythm that sounds like a clock ticking: lick-ing-tick-ing, lick-ing, tick-ing. The rhyme also creates tension, as language typically doesn't rhyme.

In the 1960s, just about everyone remembered the tagline "Winston tastes good like a cigarette should." This led to a humorous spin: "Winston tastes bad like the one I just had." The tension comes from the rhyme and the grammatical transgression—it should be ". . . *as* a cigarette should."

> **FLASH FOR YOU: This tagline don't sound no good . . .**
>
> For some audiences, problem grammar creates a flash experience of fun, dissidence, familiarity . . . depending. For others, the flash experience is defensive, outraged, or mistrustful, depending on the brand, the demographic, and the venue. What works in a blog won't resonate in an annual report.

THE INSIDE STORY

To say that the flash occurs the first time an audience sees a written message isn't accurate. The flash response on that visceral and emotional level—not merely a cognitive one—is triggered at some level with *every* communication.

So while short marketing messages such as names must provide a robust experience for the audience, longer messages, starting with taglines, have a harder task: they must sustain it. To achieve this, marketers often use strategies that bridge the divide between the audience's internal and external worlds. Here's how they do it:

Speak like a thought

Taglines frequently reflect the audience's language. *Not* the language they use when writing or even speaking, but the language of their thoughts. They're loose-jointed, easy, and repeatable. The tag for TurboTax, the online tax prep assistance product, reads, "Choose

Easy." While the consumer wouldn't say, "Choose easy" to another person, the broken construction is natural to their thoughts.

Ungrammatical wording also creates tension that generates a response in the audience. Those structures, including the American Dairy Association's famous "Got milk?" campaign, also mirror the word play in our minds: broken, in segments, yet somehow making sense. Other marketing campaigns have borrowed the line—the purest sign of a compliment. Early on, President Obama's campaign used the slogan "Got hope?" The Four Seasons Bookstore, down the block from my office, has a photo of a staff member with a mustache made from a printed page that says: "Got books?" (Each time the audience sees these lines, they flash on the milk campaign, bringing viral benefits for the milk campaign.)

Marketers also mirror the language in the audience's spoken conversation. This task requires enormous skill, as any cliché or overused statement will make the line fall flat. One message that pulled this off well was the Alka-Seltzer tagline, "I can't believe I ate the whole thing." The flash experience includes the physical sensation of being full after a big meal as well as comedic tension, since it indicates a feeling of discomfort, not a life-endangering situation like a heart attack.

Tap associations

The power of association is that the audience makes the connection themselves, without any prompting from the marketer. You can see that in these examples:

- *American Dairy Association: Behold the power of cheese.* The association is a comical but revealing one and is the flashpoint for the tagline: the word "behold." It's obviously religious, yet not overtly so, and sets up tension between "behold" and "power." What could be more powerful than God? Apparently, cheese.

- *Martha's Wardrobe: Take a Peek.* This boutique clothing shop in southern Pennsylvania features evening wear, lingerie, and fine accessories. The association is obvious, about sexuality, sensuality, and fun, and plays well with her demographic of homemakers with young children.

- *New Balance: Made in the USA.* The "Made in the USA" tagline accompanies some of the footwear company's line of running shoes, 70 percent of which are made in the United States. That distinguishes the company from major competitors like Nike and Reebok whose factory workers chug away in places like China, Thailand, and Vietnam. (The campaign even includes a documentary. Race over to *www.newbalance.com/USA* and you'll hear testimonials from Maine factory workers who use such words as "pride," "community," and, of course, "Made in the USA.")

The associations are extensive: they're about patriotism, anti-terrorism, good family values, and yes, "community" and "pride." In fact, one rendition of the tagline says "Proudly Made in the USA." Buying any other brand is practically like supporting Al-Qaeda. Still, while the company does manufacture in Maine and Massachusetts, only a quarter of their overall products are made here. The rest come from far-off places like Norway and the United Kingdom.

Create an experience

The experience can be a taste, a smell, even the feeling of motion. But the flash must have a deep physical component. One tagline that accomplishes this to a remarkable degree is that of the gaming blog site, *www.Needcoffee.com*: "We are the Internet equivalent of a triple espresso with whipped cream. Mmmm . . . whipped cream." The tag evokes the sensual powers of espresso and whipped cream, followed by the "Mmmm . . . ."

Two other examples: Nissan's *"Enjoy the ride"* and Taco Bell's *"Head for the border."* Both engage the audience in the experience of the brand, creating a flash of motion and fun. You'll notice that Taco Bell opted for that, and not a focus on taste or smell.

Create a dynamic

Marketers try to engage the audience at various levels, creating a dynamic between them. The flash can be one of curiosity or it can provoke a strong sense of tension because the message is essentially unfinished. Questions are one way of achieving this; they engage the audience but demand a response. You can think of a question as a musical note that leaves you hanging. The resolution only comes when you respond. So, we have taglines like the Dairy Association's "Got milk?" The question is rhetorical, but, being a question, demands a response. The audience has that flash of tension and curiosity, and spends a slight fraction of their time considering the message.

Humor also has an enormous dynamic quality. The flash is instant, full of tension, and uplifting.

One example is from Gizmodo—an online review of gadgets and gizmos—which uses this tagline: "So much in love with shiny new toys, it's unnatural." The other is from MightyGirl, the blog I mentioned earlier. Her tagline is "Famous Among Dozens."

FLASH FOR YOU: Test yourself

Let's go back to those taglines from your past. What do you remember most? The name? The tag? The jingle that got repeated over and over? Most likely these snippets created a flash that resonates more than your actual experience of the brand. Write down a few of these and determine what attributes, or flashpoints, resonate most. This can be instructive as you find the right name or tagline.

CREATING A TAGLINE: A CASE HISTORY

Sorrell Ridge Fruit Spread needed a market presence. But how could a small company that makes spreadable fruit products compete with Smucker's, one of the biggest jam and jelly makers around? Smucker's conjures a flash of comfort, safety, trust . . . even a scent of English muffins slathered with jam. In part, this is because of the assumptive language built into the company's tagline: "With a name like Smucker's it *has* to be good." By "good," the audience assumes they mean healthy, pure, old-fashioned goodness, although the jam is actually high in corn syrup and sugar.

The lesser-known Sorrell Ridge is the real fruit-only product. On its website, ad agency Follis describes its strategy to win customers this way:

> Go head-to-head against the competition where it was most vulnerable. Ironically, we determined that the Smucker's tagline ("With a name like Smucker's, it has to be good") was both its biggest equity and its most vulnerable target. A playful TV execution dismantled the tagline and revealed the truth: "With 100% fruit, we have to be better."

This tagline was a remarkable success. So, successful, in fact, Sorrell Ridge, now widely distributed, keeps the tagline on their label.

WebTags . . . From a Pro

Blogger Daniel Scocco supplied the Daily Blog Tips website with this selection (among others) of "The Best Website Taglines around the Internet." Here are some of them—note the tension, especially humor:

The Straight Dope: *Fighting Ignorance since 1973. (It's taking longer than we thought.)*

The Consumerist: *Shoppers bite back.*

The Superficial: *Because you're ugly.*

Scaryduck: *Not scary. Not a duck.*

The Art of Rhysisms: *Chronologically inept since 2060.*

The Breakfast Blog: *In search of the best eggs in town.*

Dooce: *Not even remotely funny.*

Shoemoney: *Skills to pay the bills.*

Oh No They Didn't!: *The celebrities are disposable, the content is priceless.*

YouTube: *Broadcast Yourself.*

Newshounds: *We watch FOX so you don't have to.*

Go Fug Yourself: *Fugly is the new pretty.*

Slashdot: *News for nerds. Stuff that matters.*

Get Rich Slowly: *Personal finance that makes cents.*

Fotolog: *Share your world with the world.*

CHAPTER 4:

Flash! Review

The name or tagline of your brand, or specific product or initiative, must accomplish several objectives:

- Say something about the content.
- Reflect your brand.
- Be effortless for the audience to remember.
- Send an invitation for the audience to join your club.
- If your products or services have separate names, they must:
  - Reflect your brand.
  - Make sense side-by-side on your webpage.
  - Be easy to say.

Make sure your tagline:

- Gets into the audience's heads
- Taps associations
- Moves quickly
- Reflects your brand language
- Conveys an immediately understandable message

5. Talk the Flash Talk

Flash is the audience's first response to a marketing message, true. But marketers must sustain the flash indefinitely. If you've ever heard a speaker at a conference, you know what I mean. The speaker makes a few jokes or tells a funny story to establish a good feeling between herself and the audience. The talk begins in earnest and, within a heartbeat, the humor is gone and the moments drag.

If marketers don't maintain the flash effect, a new flash experience of boredom, distraction, or annoyance replaces it. The hazards of this occurring are so strong, many marketers use images only. The Home Depot site shows a lineup of tractors, for example, with names but no in-depth descriptions so the message doesn't drag on.

Others use words that are purely metaphorical, regardless of whether they make sense. Think of Kissed Peach, High Endurance, and other names of deodorants. For the marketers, the less understanding, interpretation, or thought, the better. They want to concentrate the experience of the initial flash, and distill it into something that is repeated *every time* the customer sees the product.

You could argue that, paradoxically, written words in America are being reduced to pure flash. Americans read roughly one book a year. (The average varies. Some sources say women read ten books a year and men anywhere from zero to one. Others say most people read one book a year, primarily during summer vacation.) They read fewer in-depth articles than any time since the turn of the last century. Yet many spend hours each day consuming electronic forms of written communications in venues such as social networks, text messages, and Twitter, where length is measured in characters. In essence, they read messages *without actually having to read them*. The recent trend to accentuate points with graphic symbols underscores this point :).

Engage, Engage, Engage!

Regardless of the strategy, marketers create a complete flash experience by engaging the audience relentlessly—whether in a few highly charged words or a whole paragraph. This is a serious difference between marketing messages and common business writing: business writing makes the reader come to the message, while marketers put the message into the audience's head. They do this by employing the following key tactics:

CREATE A SEAMLESS FLOW OF INFORMATION

When creating a flash experience, marketers do not waste an instant of time or a fraction of space. Every word has a specific purpose, leaving behind no unanswered questions or tiny splices when the audience could pause. These "moments" are briefer than even the audience realizes. For example, this line, which might have been considered for a Long & Foster website,

The summer months at Deep Creek Lake can be enjoyed.

is in the passive voice, so it omits saying *who* can enjoy the lake. Yes, the audience knows *who* the marketer means, but only after a hairline pause, too small to notice consciously but potentially large enough to break the flash experience.

Compare that example to the real one Long & Foster used on the site:

Enjoy the summer months at Deep Creek Lake.

Marketers also avoid "dead zones": immobile, deadly clots that drain the flash experience from the body of the message. Here is another version of the Long & Foster text—also in the passive voice:

Has it been determined that another vacation is in order?

Again the dead words are unremarkable: "Has it been . . ." "is in order . . . ." These phrases create filler in an environment that demands speed. Here's what is really on the site:

Ready for another vacation?

Twitter generates a flash response in only 140 characters, and many demographics have abandoned full words for symbols ;) and letters (LOL). Or, if you're really having a great time: ROFL. In case you're not one of them, LOL means "Laughing out loud" and ROFL means "Rolling on floor laughing." Basically, both mean "ha-ha."

The seamless connection also means that message *directly* connects to the reader so the flow, from message to personal experience, is unbroken. That's why Long & Foster's example was more effective when written this way: "Ready for your next vacation?" and not "Most people are ready for a vacation right now." The content speaks to the "you" in the reader.

Facebook achieves this on its website:

Facebook is a social utility that connects you with the people around you.

Or, by using the imperative:

Use Facebook to . . .

- *keep up with friends and family*

- *share photos and videos*

- *control privacy online*

- *reconnect with old classmates*

Marketers use a more complex strategy to involve the audience in a hypothetical scenario:

Auto repair service: *"It's well after midnight. The road is empty. And dark? Really dark. Some time to have a breakdown. So, call us. We're sitting by the phone. We'll help."*

Health-care facility: "*Maybe it's a mild ache making you nervous. Or maybe you have a condition that spikes your concern. We're here. Don't take chances. Just pick up the phone and call us. Any day. Any time.*"

These examples trigger fear, one of the easiest flashes to provoke, and everyone from automobile marketers to politicians use it.

Many marketers address the audience through surrogates: people close enough in age, race, gender, interest, and other factors to safely speak for them. So, for example, Special K shows a smiling woman proclaiming, "I lost six pounds in two weeks."

The flash experience is one of empathy. The consumer thinks, "That could be me!"

FLASH FOR YOU: Secret agents

Amazingly, only select marketers value the intricacies of the written word. Even many top-notch marketing agencies delegate tasks like writing copy to lower-level employees, reserving strategic assignments to VPs. This shows in the collateral material: it's as scintillating as a trip to the dentist.

So, if you work for an agency, demand that you get some training from an expert in strategic writing who has visible successes—not a copywriter or an academic specializing in business writing.

If you hire an agency, outline your requirements for the quality and function of the writing—and insist that the agency meet these requirements or rewrite the copy at no charge to you.

USE AN EXCITING, INVITING TONE

Tone is the intonation of your voice. It can be sarcastic, for-giving, cold, or friendly. No single word creates tone, yet it is the underpinning of a prolonged flash experience. A good example of this comes from pharmaceutical companies, which wrestle with tone in their television ads. Federal regulation dictates that their warnings of side effects, which may include diarrhea, nausea, blind-ness, and other health issues most people would rather not hear or think about, are thorough and at a specific volume, so the audience can hear them.

So, marketers distract their audience in two ways. One is they show a highly animated visual in the background—a fluttering but-terfly, for example, or a couple strolling in breaking surf—to refocus the viewer's attention. And, they manage the tone of whichever actor or voiceover is reading the message. The words may say, "Severe stomach cramps and possible death . . ." but the tone is say-ing, "Trust me, I love you."

The following paragraphs use different levels of formality to shape the tone. Notice that the content never changes.

Overly Formal. *Numerous vehicles have entered cyberspace. These include blogs, podcasts, video streaming, and others. As a result, significantly more options have been created for companies wanting to get their messages to their target demographic. So, many questions may arise as to the companies' needs and capabilities in this regard, including, What medium will get their message seen by the intended demographic to yield optimum results? Our experts can and will answer these questions.*

Informal. *You know the words: blogging, podcasting, video streaming, and so many others. Yes, cyberspace has created a whole new way to reach people. But which is the best for your company? Which combinations will project the strongest message? Fuel the most enduring impression? Call or e-mail us. We'll answer these questions with clarity and confidence so you can get real-world results.*

Chatty. *You've read about blogging. Podcasting. And video streaming. So, you're wondering: What does my company need? What media will catapult my message over the hordes and leave a lasting impression on my audience? We'll help you answer these questions. Implement solutions. And get real-world results.*

The flash created by an informal or chatty tone will vary depending on the demographic: the GI and Silent Generation, raised in an age in which written communications were polite, predictable, and grammatically correct, may take offense at colloquial expressions or creative punctuation, all qualities of informal language. The flash speaks to them of irresponsibility, unprofessionalism, and worse.

On the extreme opposite end of the spectrum are the Generation Ys, also known as Generation Net. They have robust and time-consuming online lives, which—for the boys, anyway—revolve around video games. From the safety of aliases and online invisibility, they insult each other in ALL CAPS or speak in derogatory, or what other generations would see as abusive, language.

Love it, hate it, or judge it anyway you want: this tone is part of the culture, it's club language, and the initiated have a global community available at the touch of a controller.

In fact, one ad in *PC Gamer Magazine* for Runes of Magic, a site that hosts free games, tells readers: "JOIN OVER 2.5 MILLION REGISTERED USERS!" The marketing language is remarkably informal, pointed, and thick with the competitive, beat-'em-up spirit, with promises of danger and possibly death. Here's what they say:

> *Enter a world where adventure is a way of life and danger lurks around every corner. The Demon Lord has unleashed his minions in the once peaceful land of Taborea . . . . Do you have the strength, Runes stamina to be a leader?*

Another ad, for the game "Supreme Commander 2," has this headline: "THE BRAVE WILL FIGHT, BUT ONLY LEADERS WILL WIN." and offers this non-sentence alongside an image of burning rubble and the line, "A brutal civil war has shattered the friendship of three fellow officers."

This advertisement for a Sager computer notebook relies on provocative words, sentence fragments, and club-ish language:

> *Blame your little brother.*
> *Blame your high ping.*
> *But never again, blame your rig.*
> *The Segar Ultimate Gaming Machine—*
> *Built to Game. Not to Blame.*

DEVELOP STRONG SENTENCE STRUCTURE

Another way marketers create a flash experience is through sentence structure. The signs on shop windows that we discussed earlier, the ones that say "Sale! Today Only," trigger a flash of urgency. You might think the word "sale" and the time limit have fueled that flash. If so, look at this sentence: "Today, we will be holding a sale but it will be over when we close at 5:00."

The flash experience from that sentence, if there is one, is of indifference, boredom, fatigue.

One reason the first example works so well is that sentence structure mirrors the feelings in our bodies when we're feeling urgent, excited, and hurried. Think about it: your heart races, your breathing is quick and shallow, your thoughts come in short bursts, if you have thoughts at all. Now think of the short, quick bursts of "Sale! Today Only."

Another example is humor. The underlying emotion of humor is surprise, and the essence of a humorous statement is keeping the reader off-guard. According to Max Sutherland, a registered psychologist and marketing expert, our response to humor is similar to the one we feel when confronting a threat:

When something seems not quite right in an ad . . . it triggers the mind's "intruder alert" and captures attention. When humor tricks us into wrong interpretations, this same mechanism is activated to focus attention.

In the normal course of events, what we see and hear is interpreted with the mind on autopilot, in a template matching process that is conducted largely by the right brain. If the mind is on autopilot, it makes sense that the mind's eye might also have some sort of protection device—an "intruder" alarm—to alert us if the ID of something is not quite right or our interpretation of something is uncertain.

Humor triggers this attention via the same mechanism as threatening stimuli. The key difference is in how the threat is resolved. If the jolt is resolved as playful humor—a false alarm—it switches off the intruder alert instead of prompting "flight or fright." By the time the brain aborts it, however, that jolt of attention has already been felt.

Just to underscore the point I've made before: flash is about how the audience responds to messaging, not necessarily to the quality of the message itself. This is most relevant to the flash that marketers want the audience to experience when their brand is about relaxation. The Integral Yoga Institute of New York, for example, says on its site:

The chakras are powerful centers in your mind/body energy field whose subtle forces reflect the cycles of the planets above.

The sentence is as long as a deep breath, creating a flash experience of release and calm. Having a short, spirited burst of language would defeat the entire message. Notice the difference in this rewritten version:

> *The chakras. Powerful centers in your mind. In your body. In your energy field. Their forces are subtle. And, they reflect the cycles—the cycles of planets.*

Plenty of other industries rely on the calm, cool flash, even those discussing emergency procedures. The purpose is more functional than anything else: when someone's alarmed, they need to relax, think clearly, and take control. And, all this comes through in the subtle, carefully placed structure of sentences.

THE EVER-SHRINKING PARAGRAPH

It's no surprise that visuals create a strong flash experience. The swimsuit issue has sold endless copies of *Sports Illustrated* although, as far as I know, G-string bikinis have nothing to do with sports. Visuals count in print copy as well, which is one reason marketers provide limited content and short paragraphs. Thick paragraphs can create a dark and prohibitive flash experience.

I learned this almost a decade ago when I conducted a study for the Office of Personnel Management, the human resources branch of the federal government. We wanted to determine the role white space played in the time and attention job applicants gave announcements of vacancies. We expected that the applicants would have a hard time plowing through the dense text. That turned out to be true. But the big surprise was that the participants thought the announcements were angry, off-putting, and cluttered with red tape. Some said that the Feds were obviously trying to discourage outsiders from applying.

For the experimental group, we split the announcements' long paragraphs into short clusters. We didn't change the content and only changed words to include transitions. A significantly higher number of participants thought the announcements were friendly and accessible.

Marketers use another device to give the appearance of brevity: headlines and sidebars. You see this on websites, where short chunks of content are set off in shaded columns and boxes. These elements create a flash experience that's energetic, with strong, sparse language zeroing in on the most provocative words.

Here is an example of a web piece. Notice the difference between the header, with the flashpoints on "body" and "athlete," and the flatter language in the following paragraph. It's from the Nike website:

If you have a body, you are an athlete.

When Nike co-founder Bill Bowerman made this observation many years ago, he was defining how he viewed the endless possibilities for human potential in sports. He set the tone and direction for a young company called Nike, and today those same words inspire a new generation of Nike employees.

The headline creates the flash experience: without it the audience might ignore the message. Nike, with its all-energy brand, continues to infuse the paragraph with energy—not as intensely as the headline, but present with the words "endless possibilities" and "inspire."

The Search Engine Caveat

The search engine has created a strange challenge for marketing writers. Unlike other venues, the search engine is about "whoever gets there first wins." In this case, "there" is the first half of the first page on the site. How marketers get there is another matter: by the amount of hits on a website, the number of unique visitors it gets, the click-through rate, and other metrics.

So, marketers must determine how to position key search engine words on the site.

The words in the headlines have more search engine clout than those in the narrative. This presents an interesting problem in terms of flash: the words the search engine wants, the ones most people key in when they're searching, are usually mundane, and so, low in flash possibility.

For example, runners who want footwear will probably key in "running," "shoes." If they want a specific brand, they'll key in that.

To satisfy the search engine and the audience's need for a flash experience, marketers rely on the principle of distraction. They add visuals, sound, and videos, and surround the search words with exciting and exacting words.

Key In . . .

To get a sense of how marketers tap into the leveraging power of search engines, key in "running shoes." You'll immediately see names such as Roadrunner Sports (how better to capture the possibilities of search engines than embed the search word in your name?), New Balance, and Saucony. Then, go these websites and look at the headings. Some are better than others but even the most mundane are cast in a high-energy tone.

Show, Show, Show . . .

There's a maxim in the communications world: "Show, don't tell."
With telling, the audience must rely on the marketer's insights.
This creates a buffer between the audience and the message, and
the flash experience is significantly weakened. If marketers show,
the audience experiences the message for themselves. The difference is between telling someone "Deep Creek Lake is nice" and
showing them "Deep Creek Lake has glistening water surrounded
by dense hardwood forests." That's one reason YouTube has taken
off as an advertising tool. The audience is involved on a passive
level: no words to read, no scrolling down a page, and the effect
is absorbing.

Still, words are not entirely a thing of the past. Neither is
Roto-Rooter, a company founded in the 1930s. The jingle and
lyrics—"Call Roto-Rooter, that's the name, and away go trou-
bles down the drain"—is legendary in the marketing universe
and could be one reason for the brand's enduring success. On
the website, the audience hears the jingle, which creates a flash
experience of warmth, security, nostalgia, and familiarity. Then,
they see this:

> *Need a Plumber?*
>
> *Trusted and recommended since 1935, Roto-Rooter is the
> largest provider of plumbing and drain cleaning services in North
> America. Our plumbers are available 24 hours a day, 7 days a
> week.*

The "telling part" is embedded in the first line: "Trusted and
recommended . . . ." Then comes the "show" part: "since 1935."
The audience associates longevity with being "trusted and recommended." The advertisement goes on to say: "Roto-Rooter is the

largest provider of plumbing and drain cleaning services in North America." Once again, the power of this claim is the association: a large company must be good.

The line isn't pithy or edgy, but that's not the flash the marketers want. The toilet is overflowing. The bathroom is a mess and water's gushing from the ceiling to the living room below. You want reassurance. You want calm. You want a grandpa in overalls to stop by with a wrench. Trusted and recommended since 1935. Your plumber. Your gramps.

Roto-Rooter's ad also underscores an illogical aspect of audience response. Just because the company's been around since 1935 ultimately means nothing. The audience also feels excited about new brands, although they may be untested (think Vista), feel reassured by large firms (think Arthur Andersen), trust old ones (think Lehman Brothers), or believe in trendy ones (think Enron).

But marketing is about feeling, and sticking around since 1935 means a lot.

Do Good in a Flash

Charitable and grassroots organizations have a dilemma. In telling about a dire situation, they risk being schmaltzy or syrupy and alienating the audience. For all her good intentions, for example, Sally Struthers's pleas for the Christian Children Fund, now known as ChildFund International, have been a source of parody and mocking references for decades.

Recently, though, marketers have become adept at creating a "soft" flash experience based on sorrow, empathy, and longing, by showing situations and not telling about them. In the process, they distance themselves from the message, enabling the audience to experience it for themselves.

One example is the 2008 Olympics "Giving is Winning" campaign. The object was to get sports supplies, such as uniforms, to refugees in camps around the globe. Skeptics might think: How about food? Hospital supplies? Better sanitation? Why sports supplies?

The marketers anticipate these questions and underscore the importance of their cause by describing teenagers, restless in the best of circumstances, who are cooped up in refugee camps with nothing to do. Here's what they say in one announcement, which simultaneously reported that the United Arab Emirates will be participating in the project:

Rwanda: clothes to pursue dreams

More than 50,000 people are in refugee camps in Rwanda. And almost 62 per cent are under 17 years old. These youngsters are particularly in need of leisure activities to overcome the idleness of their life in a camp but also of items such as clothing, which counts a lot to the welfare of a refugee. This is why the Dubai International Humanitarian City (DIHC), a global humanitarian and aid hub from United Arab Emirates, has decided to join the IOC-UNHCR campaign. Its donation of about 19,000 items of sport and casual clothing for men, women and children have been recently distributed in four different camps in Rwanda: Nkamira Transit Centre (hosting 2,163 refugees from North Kivu, Democratic Republic of Congo) . . . .

The marketers *show* the situation: younger people outnumber older ones who would discipline them; boredom that can lead to violence; deprivation is so great in the camps that the inhabitants hardly have clothing. Any emotional embroidery on these simple facts would turn this marketing effort into a Hallmark card of the worst variety.

Later in this book, we'll discuss the recent phenomenon of "cause marketing," in which companies market causes, rather than their own brands. These efforts may bring good to the world. But their mission is not entirely altruistic: they get immense marketing value from it as the audience associates the companies' names with good work.

BEFORE AND AFTER

Perhaps the most common example of "show, don't tell" is also among the most misleading: marketing messages targeting weight loss. The marketers show "before" and "after" pictures. This strategy is more than a simple comparison. The audience thinks the woman in the "after" picture looks slimmer when they view the "before" picture first. If they looked at the "after" picture on its own, the effect would be less convincing.

The same dynamic exists with words. Marketers help the audience *see* the message for themselves with clear and specific words. On its box, Special K tells us:

I lost six pounds in two weeks.

Six pounds in two weeks is a lot for any audience. True, the audience doesn't see the "before," but they don't need to. Their own experience with failed diets and frustration at seeing the size of their clothes increase is enough.

Most significantly, the messaging is aspirational, creating an upbeat, hopeful, and energized flash experience. This flash creates a misleading message. In a less conspicuous part of the page, ad, or box is a qualifier reading something like this: "These results are not typical." The audience, blinded by the halo effect, doesn't care or even notice it.

CHAPTER 5:

Flash! Review

To create a flash experience for the audience—one that endures and carries your brand—your written communications must do the following:

- Leverage space
- Create a seamless flow of information
- Address the audience directly
- Manage the tone of the message
- Use sentence structure to create a flash experience
- Limit the size of your paragraphs and the amount of text
- Show and don't tell
- Embed your search words in headers and subheads

Use plain language

- Active voice
- Concise word use
- Informal tone
- Cohesive structure

6. Advertising . . . And the Flash Goes On

No question, advertising has played a pivotal role in American commerce. Traditionally, ads had a Hollywood-style edge with jingles, creative taglines, and stars and starlets practically swooning over the brand. Advertising was the first place brands captured the potential of flash communications. The power of ads endures today. From television shorts to billboards to endorsements at sporting events, they account for a large number of the 5,000–7,000 messages Americans receive each day. Advertisements are core shapers of our culture and are ensuring their future by morphing with the times.

One example is billboards. Until recently these were stagnant since the cost and effort of changing them was too consuming. One billboard would remain in place for months. And, because the audience saw them when rushing along the road, their effectiveness was negligible.

Outdoor Advertising: The Perks

According to BPS Outdoor Media billboards bring these advantages:

- More people can view one particular billboard than the Super Bowl! (The billboard must be located in a high traffic area like most Interstate billboards.)
- Billboards are viewed 24 hours a day, 7 days a week by billions of different people.
- Outdoor Advertising Association of America did a study in 1999 that says people glance at 70 percent of the billboards they pass. Of these billboards, 63 percent are actually read.
- Billboards reach 93 percent of all Americans.
- Outdoor advertising costs 80 percent less than television advertising, 60 percent less than newspaper ads, and 50 percent less than radio advertisements.

As for volume:

- There are 53 percent more automobiles and 102 percent more road trips over the past years.
- The number of traveling and household vehicles has risen six times faster than the population rate.
- According to a study by Arbitron, people are spending less time reading and watching television because they are spending more time traveling to and from work. The average American is in a car for fifteen hours per week!

But communications companies are getting smart from their computers. And billboards are becoming interactive. For example, Honda has a billboard for its Civic showcasing an image of the car. When the audience sends a message through a cell phone to the number listed on the screen, the car starts up, smoke bursts from the tailpipe, and the tail lights blink.

On his blog, neuromarketing expert Roger Dooley says:

> *I think this ad works at two levels. Most obviously, there's the novelty of being able to make a billboard do something. Most outdoor ads are entirely static, and the fact that this one changes its status in response to a text message is startling and intriguing.*

From a neuromarketing perspective, this billboard also conveys a subtle "ownership" message that might increase the probability of a sale. Research has shown that touching or holding an object can be enough to produce this effect. To me, it seems likely that "starting" the Honda in the billboard might well do the same. This . . . certainly seems much better than looking at a mere picture of the car.

Marketers also extend the flash experience by getting the audience not only to turn on the car, but to *commit* to turning on the car. They are no longer mere observers of the ad but participants on their own terms. This relationship is reinforced every time they see the Honda billboard. The buzz factor is certainly at work here, as well: people tell their friends. The more excited they are, the greater the carryover flash.

Billboards also point to the hazards of advertising. With websites, YouTube videos, and e-newsletters, the audience can choose whether or not to engage in the message. With billboards—as with some other forms of marketing—the message is unavoidable. Some may like it and others don't. And some who don't are complaining. For example, the Coalition to Ban Billboard Blight is fighting what it considers ugly billboards in the Los Angeles area. Here's what they say on their website:

> *The Coalition to Ban Billboard Blight is a non-profit 501(c)(4) organization representing groups and individuals committed to defending*

the urban landscape of Los Angeles against billboards and other forms of
outdoor advertising that blight our public spaces.

Our mission includes education, outreach, and political and legal
action to protect citizens' rights to walk and drive their streets and congre-
gate in public areas without a constant assault of advertising messages. We
welcome all forms of support—money, volunteer time, letter-writing—to
help us in this fight. The visual landscape of the city belongs to everyone,
not just the advertising companies who want to use it as a canvas for their
commercial messages. Please help us protect and defend it.

This presents an interesting dilemma for marketers. The flash experience is about the venue as well as the brand. If the audience dislikes billboards, for example, the flash response of negativity, defensiveness, and outrage probably will carry over to the brand. Even the carryover flash from news articles, bloggers, and general buzz about the debate will influence their experience.

But, it's undeniable that some billboards can become cultural icons. One of the most famous is the "Citgo" sign in Boston, Massachusetts, first erected in 1945. This sixty-foot-by-sixty-foot sign holds 5,878 neon lights and has been on since it first went live in 1965, with hiatuses during energy crises. Today, though, the Citgo sign is a tourist destination just outside another relic: Fenway Park.

How Bad Are They?

Advertisements are up front. The brands are selling a product. They're wooing the audience. And in a day when marketers pose as bloggers, brands searching for new customers become social network "'friends,'" and product representatives leave comments on websites as if they were objective parties, advertisements—at least the authentic ones—could be the most honest forms of marketing around.

More on the Love/Hate of Advertisements

At one time, the role of an advertisement was pretty much black and white—it defined the brand, was generally stagnant, and brought in customers. Now, though, the audience is weary of advertising, as demonstrated in a Yankelovich Partners poll of consumers for the American Association of Advertising Agencies, as reported by the *New York Times*:

- 65 percent said they get hit by too much advertising.
- 61 percent said marketing and advertising "is out of control."
- 60 percent said their view of advertising is more negative than before.
- 54 percent said they actually "avoid buying products that overwhelm them with advertising and marketing."
- 69 percent said they "are interested in products and services that would help them skip or block marketing."

As for television ads, people are finding ways to avoid them through DVRs, TiVo, the "mute" button, and bathroom breaks. In response, some marketers are considering alternatives such as blogger outreach and a presence on social networking sites.

Yet, the blogging universe is cluttered, and social networks such as Facebook are great for connecting to friends, but not to businesses and customers. So, marketers are drifting back to television advertising, encouraged by the flash success of some campaigns.

One example is the GEICO car insurance ads. They're consistently funny and self-mocking. GEICO's spokesperson is a smart-talking gecko (with an English, or is it Australian, accent!). Another campaign uses the tagline "So easy, even a caveman can do it." The campaign creates an enduring and memorable flash experience, tapping humor, familiarity, and relationship.

Further, while most online marketers measure their success by page views or buzz, the GEICO ads clearly translated into profits. Mike Hughes, president and creative director of the Martin Agency, which is the company that developed the ads, says,

> When GEICO started with us, they were spending probably just one or two million [on advertising]. They've had three million new customers last year, they're the fastest growing car insurance, and I don't think it's revealing too much to say they spend in the hundreds of millions of dollars . . . because it pays like crazy.

Marketers have sometimes made ads a springboard for longer campaigns that create an active, engaging event for the audience. The longer their engagement, the longer and more repeated the flash experience. This can win marketers new customers *and* brand loyalty.

FLASH FOR YOU: Is advertising right for you?

Advertising, as part of a larger campaign, can be helpful. Before you invest, consider these questions:

- Will your advertisement entertain or otherwise engage the audience?
- Can your ad create a positive flash experience?
- Can you repeat the ad often enough (in numerous iterations) for the audience to remember it?
- Does the ad give your audience a good reason to respond appropriately?

When Negativity Hits . . .

The marketing climate demands engrossing campaigns. But what happened when those campaigns creative negative buzz? Does the carryover flash devastate the brand? Tarnish other marketing efforts? Advertising agency Crispin Porter & Bogusky has mastered the art (if you can call it that) of attracting controversy: the agency's response is even more interesting than its tactics.

The agency was the brains behind Burger King's "subservient chicken" campaign. This stunt was meant to create buzz about the fast-food chain's chicken products, marked by the tagline "Chicken, just the way you like it." The subservient chicken works like this: First the audience goes online to *www.subservientchicken.com* to a living room with a television, couch, and so on—presumably belonging to a college student or a twenty-something person—in other words, Burger King's demographic.

There, the viewer sees a person dressed in a chicken costume. In a box just beneath it, he can type in a command such as drinking, squatting, pecking the ground, and dancing. The chicken does what he asks . . . almost. If the viewer types in something risqué, the chicken shakes an admonishing chicken finger. If the viewer asks the chicken to eat at, say, McDonald's, the chicken sticks its chicken finger down its throat.

The campaign generated massive amounts of buzz—yet, word around the blogosphere was mixed. Bloggers complained that the subservient chicken was just a stunt that had virtually no connection to the brand. Others commented that the campaign was more appealing, or at least memorable, than the sandwich. The overarching sentiment was that the campaign brought plenty of attention to itself but not a whole lot to the client.

Crispin Porter & Bogusky launched another campaign, the Burger King "virgin tasters." The marketing crew trekked across the world in search of populations who had never eaten a burger, or, for that matter, heard of them. This took them to the Inuit of the Icelandic tundra, Chang Mai villagers from northern Thailand, and Transylvanian peasants of Romania. In the documentary-style taste test, vaguely reminiscent of the Pepsi challenge of the 1980s, participants dressed in their best native garb, and compared Burger King's burger to McDonald's. Guess who won?

The ad met with splendid controversy that won Burger King prime spots everywhere from blog sites to news networks. Critics from world health experts to advertising pundits accused Burger King of being condescending to native populations, pushing the worst of imperialism onto unknowing tribes, and force-feeding third-world inhabitants meals rich in salt and fat instead of more nutritious alternatives.

Burger King's response has been low key and vaguely liberal: they say they worked with local authorities, tribal leaders, and others in creating the ad. They were sensitive to cultural norms. And the inhabitants lived in areas where food was bountiful.

As for Crispin Porter & Bogusky, in an interview with *Advertising Age* in December 2008, Rob Reilly, co-executive creator and partner of the agency said:

> *Advertising is designed to be talked about, and hopefully people will notice it . . . I'm not surprised that people are writing about* [*"Whopper Virgins"*] *positive or negative, because that's the design of how we approach things as an agency.*

He went on to say:

We go into every project thinking: Is it an idea that the press—and not necessarily the advertising press—will write about? If it's not, maybe it's not such a good idea.

One of the most difficult issues marketers must address, regardless of venue, is the frequency of the ad campaign. One advertisement rarely brings in customers even when it's announcing a sale or special offer. Yet, too many ads can create so-called audience wear-out; the audience sees the advertisement so frequently it tips the saturation point and the flash experience wears off.

According to Mark Levit, managing partner of Partners & Levit Advertising New York and a professor of marketing at New York University:

To understand why wearout occurs, scientists studied the brain to understand cognitive thinking and responses to these situations. They found the brain tends to ignore an object or theme that's repeated too many times. Essentially, most communication works by triggering memories. Old images or concepts are associated with something in the advertisement, recognizing elements as familiar. In the process, something new may be introduced and the brain links it with the old. When something new or unknown to a customer is presented to the brain for processing it evaluates: a) whether it is new and b) whether it corresponds to prior experience, knowledge and beliefs. The familiar portion of the advertisement is treated more casually. The brain recognizes it and spends less time evaluating its validity. It's interpreted as given . . . .

But the plot thickens. Marketers also report that rather than prompt a positive or even indifferent response, an ad can cause the audience reaction to grow sour. The flash becomes negative, signaling that the brand is dull, done, or even obnoxious.

FLASH FOR YOU: Timing is everything

When advertising, one of the most critical issues you need to address is the frequency of your ad campaign. One advertisement rarely brings in customers, even when it's announcing a sale or special offer. Besides, you're not trying to get a one-time customer. You are trying to help people own your brand and purchase your product or service for the long term. So, your advertising strategy must tap into numerous media and venues, launching simultaneous television and online ads, for example, and placing your ad in a predictable spot each time.

ADVERTISING HOT SPOTS

One of the greatest challenges marketers confront is finding space for an advertisement. And, they're getting adept at finding new ways to do it, virtually and physically. Here are some of the most common ones:

Magazines

People, especially women, spend more time with magazines than newspapers or online publications. They flip through them on the train to work, for example, and pick them up a few days later while relaxing at home. So, they continuously see the message, and the flash experience repeats.

Marketers also apply the "usability" strategy; that is, making their ads "usable." For example, *Ladies' Home Journal* offered a recipe for one of Keebler's "Ready Crust Creations," called "Minty Grasshopper Pie." It contained cream cheese, sweetened condensed milk, and fudge cookies (tastes great, and what better way to simultaneously induce a heart attack *and* diabetes?). The brand, in this case Keebler, seems to be selling a recipe, and its pie shells are just another ingredient.

Recipes like these create a *total* flash experience:

- **Relevance.** The recipe is relevant to the magazine, which is all about food and home. The carryover flash helps create legitimacy and authenticity.
- **Relationship.** The recipe, with images of happy children and family, connects the treats to being loved.
- **Senses.** The image, the name—Minty Grasshopper Pie—and the recipe itself tap smell, touch (heat from the oven), and taste.

As for the usability factor: the audience can *use* the recipe to make tasty desserts and, while they're at it, win the love of their families. They may clip the recipe, pass it on to friends, and return to it, a repeated form of advertising without the wear-out. They also associate Keebler's with the recipe (in fact, any pie crust will suffice—in fact, some may be cheaper). The flash experience is deeply engrained to the point of becoming *flash memory*. This is an ideal place: how many millions of women make chocolate chip cookies for their children using Nestle Toll House Morsels every time, when any substitute, even smashed-up chocolate candy bars, will work just as well?

Interestingly, some marketers have forsaken magazine ads, although readership is actually increasing, according to *Media Life Magazine*. And, while old standards such as the venerable *Gourmet Magazine* are dying, new publications are appearing all the time.

FLASH FOR YOU: The usability factor

Creating an ad campaign that has a high usability factor is an excellent way to create a meaningful campaign. Tips, insightful facts, and links to related services will all engage the audience. Some marketers also use "giveaways": those pens, squeezy balls, and other trinkets that you see in stunning quantities in booths at conferences. Giveaways aren't a bad idea, but make sure they're related to your brand and reinforce the flash experience triggered by your other marketing efforts. Too often you see Washington, D.C.–based consultants giving away beach balls, visitor centers giving away key chains, and just about everyone giving away pens.

Online venues

Marketers are entranced with online advertising for reasons that have more to do with numbers than the realities of flash. For example, they can track how many visitors click on a display or graphic ad (presumably to become customers) and pay for the ads accordingly. According to one *New York Times* article, about a third of online advertising budgets goes to these ads, but the numbers will soon be dwindling:

> *Roughly a third of all online ad spending goes to such ads, yet Internet users are increasingly reluctant to click on them.*

Another factor, which we addressed briefly when discussing billboards, is that the venue should create a flash experience that carries over to the audience. This problem has been hitting the online universe hard. Ironically, one reason is the flash that marketers themselves experience about online advertising. It's new, which creates the flash experience of excitement, expectation, and hope. It's also an exclusive club they want to join: the fast-paced, ahead-of-the-crowd digital set. Yet, because it's new, it's also untested.

One example is pre-rolls, the ads that run before online videos. From the marketers' perspective, pre-rolls present an opportunity for the audience to experience the message while their attention is fresh. And, because they can't fast-forward, they're basically captive. But the audience is growing increasingly impatient with pre-rolls. According to an article in BizReport, the publication for online marketers:

> *The main issue with pre-roll ads is that, on the whole, they can't be skipped, forcing the viewer to sit through them. In an age of immediacy, many viewers just don't have the patience or the will to sit through 15 or 30 seconds of content they didn't request . . . pre-rolls caused consumers to click away. They found that almost 16 percent would abandon a video rather than sit through pre-roll ads. On newspaper and magazine sites that number was higher at 25 percent.*

FLASH FOR YOU: A little bit of research
A little bit of research should help you find the best place to reach your audience with an advertisement. But before you invest, take these steps:

Look at how similar ads position their offerings. What is the tone, the look, and the promise?

Call the companies who placed the ads and ask about their return, when appropriate. You don't have to contact competitors, but a business in a related field or with a similar demographic can help.

Determine what you want the audience to do. Your objective may not be to get them to purchase your product. Instead, you may want them to attend an event they'll buzz about and bring other people to attend, or to go to your website.

Track the response rate. If online, you will have an easier time, especially if you want the audience to go to your website or purchase online. If not, ask customers how they heard about you.

Try different approaches and wait. You'll need to advertise for a few months before you can be certain about the effectiveness of your efforts.

Newspapers

For the past decade or so, newspaper advertising has had a bad rap, equaled only by the bad rap given to the actual newspapers. Mori Research tells a different story. In a report discussing the advertising power of newspapers, they wrote: "This research finds that almost two-thirds of American adults actively check advertising at least weekly for things they might want to buy." The report went on to say that half of ad viewers check in on Sunday. Saturday is a little less popular, Wednesday and Friday are at 13 percent each, and the other days are pretty low.

Here are some other facts from Mori Research:

- Fifty-three percent of adults used newspapers to make a shopping or purchase decision in the previous 30 days, while 27 percent used the Internet, which now is the second-leading source.
- High-income ($100K+) shoppers and young adults favor the Internet as a primary advertising source.
- Half of adults have received, through mail or home delivery within the last thirty days of the survey, a free shopper publication with preprints, and 42 percent of adults said they had received one in the previous week. Three-fourths of those who receive these publications say they read at least some of the advertising inserts that come with them.

Finally, Mori tells us that one of the most successful advertisements is the coupon. Here's what the firms says:

Almost half of consumers regularly or occasionally save non-grocery coupons. Two-thirds of coupon savers prefer newspapers for coupon delivery (mostly on Sundays). Consumers in the $50,000 to $99,000 income range are active in saving coupons as well.

Newspapers offer marketers another benefit or deficit, depending on the circumstances: carryover flash. An advertisement can be compromised if it's beside a photo of a car crash or some other tragedy. Similarly, advertisements trying to engender a flash response of excitement about, say, an upcoming sale or product launch will be thwarted if surrounded by other sale ads.

But the reverse is also true. For example, the "Home" section of the publication typically features lush gardens and perfect landscapes with an advertisement for a fertilizer beside it. The flash generated by the beautiful garden carries over to the advertisement.

Television

Like newspaper ads, TV ads are tricky, and advertisers are nervous about them. That means networks have space to fill and will give advertisers special deals or even freebies. The problem with this generosity is wear-out. The audience sees the advertisement once, twice, the brain essentially says forget it, and annoyance sinks in.

As we mentioned before, one reason for television's diminishing power is DVRs. According to one TiVo researcher, 30 percent of all households have TiVo or some other means of controlling their television viewing time. Most viewers fast-forward through ads at some point—according to the researcher's calculation, only one-third actually watch the ads.

So, why do brands advertise? Television still offers advantages other media forms don't. It can create brand celebrity (think Frank Perdue), provide entertainment (think GEICO caveman) and, since television is a relatively big screen in today's BlackBerry-sized screen world, has credibility.

According to the TiVo researcher, "Traditional TV advertising is alive and well even in DVR households." The effectiveness depends on the show. Viewers fast-forward commercials in shows like *24*, *Lost*, and *House*, but stay during *American Idol*. He added another point, which underscores the significance of targeting demographics: the most-watched advertisements are from pharmaceutical companies. While most viewers may not like the message (or the litany of warnings that follow) the ones who remain are captive, eager to find solutions for ailments that devastate their lives or the life of someone close to them.

FLASH FOR YOU: Got TV?

If television seems like the right choice for you, remember:

More focused is better than more people. Pick the best cable station and the best time, depending on who's watching and why.

Most television spots are thirty seconds. These generate leads and can get your audience to your website. But they don't sell products. For that, a sixty-second spot is significantly better.

Flash or otherwise state your web address and toll-free number on the screen at least three times, or have it on throughout the advertisement.

Give them something specific to respond to: a special sale; a unique event; a new, but limited, product.

Shop around for the best production company. Review its other ads. Call its customers and ask if the company was easy to work with, customer-oriented, and creative.

Where else?

The space available for marketing messages is shrinking as the universe of marketing is expanding. As I mentioned at the start of this chapter, marketers are becoming increasingly adept at filling that space. Josh Kopelman, for example, founded the company Half.com, discussed earlier. He recently thought up another venture called "Jingle Networks" after discovering that each time you dial 411, the phone company makes approximately 90 percent profit. That's a lot of money, seeing that people make six billion phone calls a year, making it an $8 billion business.

With Jingle Networks, you can get free directory assistance simply by dialing 1-800-Free-411. How does that connect to advertising? Kopelman charges companies to advertise on the 1-800-Free-411 number.

US Airways now has advertisements for the OnStar navigation system on its tray tables. AirTran offers seventeen Coca-Cola products—that's seventeen—with ads on its napkins and cups. JetBlue offers ever more advertising platforms, thanks to its in-air TV screens.

Dove soap, which claims to be bringing self-esteem to women everywhere, is involved, too. JetBlue passed out samples of Dove products, which were also advertised on Channel 13, the flight-tracking channel. Plenty of airlines now accept advertising on ticket jackets, cocktail napkins, and airsickness bags, (people are getting sick less frequently and using them to deposit chewed up wads of gum and other debris).

How well do these advertising efforts work? According to the *New York Times*, almost 90 percent of the passengers who saw advertisements sponsored by the Quebec Department of Tourism on US Airlines flights could remember some of the ad; 54 percent remembered the name of the advertisement; and 7.5 percent remembered the website.

FLASH FOR YOU: Where to go marketing

Finding an effective spot for your ad depends on the demographic, the flash experience you want your audience to take from your message, and the flash carryover they may get from the venue. Plenty of advertising is guess, of course, so it can't hurt to take risks. Here are some unusual possibilities.

Soaps. Put your logo on the back of a bar of soap or on the inner wrapper.

Wrappers. The inside of most wrappers are blank. Use these as a spot for a contest or quiz. Have the audience go to your website for the answer and the prize. This will lengthen their experience with your brand and help seal the relationship.

Plastic newspaper bags. Those thin bags that homeowners see in the morning as they retrieve their newspaper from the elements are more persuasive than you might think. According to Mori, "Half of newspaper subscribers have seen plastic delivery bags, and half of them, or one-fourth of subscribers, said they usually read the ads."

Write a list of five or ten unique places where you can advertise; be as creative or outrageous as possible. Then go back and consider the possibilities of each.

Product placement

The audience's skepticism about advertising has created another marketing phenomenon: product placement. This strategy, wherein marketers embed their brand into a movie or television show, is one of the fastest-growing forms of advertising, outselling traditional ads. Its power is entirely based on carryover flash. The audience sees a celebrity they admire driving a car or enjoying a brand of food and experiences second-hand, or vicarious, flash.

Researchers have studied product placement to determine whether it works and why.

In a paper presented at the annual meeting of the International Communication Association, researcher Seoyoon Choi explains that product placement may work on three psychological levels. One occurs because "good feelings associated with the scene are transferred to the brand." The second is called "mere exposure theory . . . ."

Viewers develop favorable feelings toward a brand simply because they are repeatedly exposed to the brand. This seems especially true for brands presented as props in several movie scenes.

She adds that product placement also transforms the audience's experience of using a product so it becomes

. . . richer, warmer, more exciting, and/or more enjoyable . . . the product is not merely seen in a functional sense but becomes part of the story context and is endowed with characteristics associated with the movie.

Third, Choi says, when the audience recognizes and identifies a message as an ad

. . . they process it differently than they would if they were unaware of its commercial intent. Compared to classical advertising, product placement is less likely to be recognized as persuasive, and thus prevents viewers from counterarguing, scrutinizing, or rejecting the message.

The list of product placement ads is increasing, and most television shows and movies are loaded with them. For example, the movie *Sex and the City* featured Adidas, American Airlines, Chanel, Christian Dior, Cup Noodles, Dell, Diane von Furstenberg, Dove, Hermès, Hershey's, M&Ms, Motorola, Netflix, *New York Magazine*, Pantene, Prada, Smartwater, Sony, Sprint, Starbucks, Swarovski, Tiffany & Co., *TV Guide*, U-Haul, Uniden, Van Cleef & Arpels, Vera Wang, Versace, VitaminWater, Vivienne Westwood, and *Vogue*, among others.

But does product placement work? The answer is yes and no. Product placement can create the critical flash experience *if* the relationship between the product and plot is strong, *if* the message taps numerous senses such as sight and sound, and *if* it creates a strong and enduring flash experience.

A classic example is from the movie *ET*, where the extraterrestrial was lured out of hiding by a trail of Reese's Pieces. No mere logo-on-a-wrapper flashing before our eyes; Reese's played a heroic role in getting the plot, and the animated character, moving.

More recently, in the 2006 show *Miracle Workers* on ABC, CVS made a product placement splash by footing the medicine bill for patients' post-surgery. You'll notice CVS wasn't just a brand on a screen but the benevolent pharmacy, stirring the feelings of trust the audience yearns for when filling prescriptions.

It's likely, however, that the effectiveness of product placement is already degenerating. As you may recall, research shows that advertising works better when the audience isn't aware they're viewing an ad. In other words, the experience, as we discussed earlier, must be seamless.

Today's audiences are becoming increasingly aware of product placement ads. Rather than melding into the backdrop of their movie, TV show, or other production, product placement ads pull the audience *out of the story* as they are aware someone's marketing to them.

Further, consumer advocates have become actively engaged in efforts to halt product placement. For example, in the 2008 movie *Iron Man*, the title character, played by Robert Downey Jr., had just escaped captivity from terrorists. As he stepped off the plane in his homeland, one of his first requests was an all-American cheeseburger. Soon after, he was eating one of them, the Burger King logo in plain view.

The fast-food chain's marketers knew that after seeing the movie the flash experience would trigger as kids passed Burger King. They'd clamor to go in and their parents would oblige them. But Burger King wasn't only the burger of choice for Iron Man—the chain also distributed Iron Man toys. This led to a new round of carryover flash as the children's friends saw the new toys.

That campaign won enormous criticism from parent groups, including the Campaign for a Commercial-Free Childhood (CCFC), which accused the ad of promoting obesity in kids. In its news release the organization said, "Even as childhood obesity and youth violence are significant public health problems, a major fast food company and a major motion picture studio are working together to promote junk food and violence to children."

Not exactly the kind of buzz you want to have. It's worth noting that Burger King has addressed this age-old issue before—and probably has how many times since?

The CCFC's efforts might not have stopped parents from taking their kids to the movie or even Burger King. But it does create informational buzz about product placement and create momentum that will most likely influence future marketing campaigns.

FLASH FOR YOU: TV continued: How 'bout that product placement?

You can get exposure through "product placement" in a meaningful way through the media and in community events. Here are some ideas:

Embed your message in local events. This concept is standard fare in sports events, where the sponsor's name is plastered over uniforms, bikes, racing cars, or other types of equipment. This gives the brand repeat exposure. Most likely the flash response is not because of the event itself. Instead, it's about belonging: by sponsoring a play, for example, the brand becomes one of the audience's inner circle, sharing their values and tastes.

Do product placement on cable TV. Cable television is another example of a flash experience based in feelings of belonging. In winter months, many cable stations offer updates about road conditions and school closings. So, the audience might see an on-the-scene reporter wearing a scarf with a brand's logo, or the anchor could be sipping coffee from a branded cup.

Integrate your product into how-to's. Community centers often offer home improvement classes; chefs of varying degrees of celebrity post cooking videos on YouTube; and adult education classes offer a range of programs. You may be able to get your product in these venues for free. In the process, you'll also be "seeding": enabling the audience to use your product, and assuming they like it, creating buzz.

Integrating Those Products!

Product integration is like product placement on steroids. Unlike product placement, in which the brand slips into scenes, product integration allows the brand to weave in and out. It appears in the hands of actors, for example, then reappears in the advertisements shown during the program, then shows up in contests, DVDs, and other venues.

The purpose, as with product placement, is to create an "organic" or "natural" association between the show and the brand. In other words, the audience isn't *aware* of the brand, but they are affected nonetheless. What marketers are hoping for is "invisible flash": the audience responds but on such a low level they may not even realize they're responding. If they see the brand often enough, though, it quietly becomes part of their memory.

CHAPTER 6:

Flash! Review

Here are the core considerations about how—and whether—to approach an advertising campaign:

How much of your budget you can devote to your advertising campaign.

The venues where your demographic gets information. These include:

- Magazines
- Social networks
- Online or traditional radio and television
- Newspapers

The flash response you want from your ads in the short term and long term.

Your experience with previous efforts.

PART 3

SECONDHAND FLASH

7. One Person's Opinion: Flash and Carryover Flash

So far we've been discussing the flash effect that occurs when the audience directly encounters a marketing message. They may see an advertisement on television, confront a pre-roll online, or hear a jingle as they enter a website. How they respond depends on a number of variables, including the venue (a billboard); the context (a newspaper ad with stories around the demographic—think G33K); and the timing.

Increasingly, marketers seek to influence consumers indirectly as well as directly. This is called carryover flash. A widespread method of creating carryover flash is through articles in magazines, newspapers, or online. With articles, especially in publications, the flash can be indirect or beyond the brander's control. For instance, consider these factors:

1. **The publication.** If a consultant publishes in the *Harvard Business Review*, the carryover is one of trust, admiration, and importance. If the publication is *Slate*, the carryover flash may be associated with energy and style.

2. **The positioning.** Where the article, or link to the article, appears will significantly affect the flash it generates. Front or homepage status creates a flash experience that's about status and credibility and enhances the number of readers.

3. **The venue.** If the publication is online, the brand can heighten its search engine ranking and tap a prequalified audience.

4. **The style.** Publications generally have a style that reflects their brand and not the author's. Some editors adjust the text to accommodate this, while others don't. Regardless, most add headlines that create the initial flash and create a halo effect for the entire article.

But another factor is at work: the author cannot speak directly about his brand, because doing so would make the article an advertisement. So, the authors need to discuss related subjects, positioning themselves as experts. The connection between expert and brand is thin, and the marketing value negligible. Only when authors place their publications on their own branded websites do they achieve any real benefit.

FLASH FOR YOU: Publish or perish or what?

Whether an article will bring its author customers is questionable. But writing articles still has immense value. They can support your collateral material and help your search engine ranking. Equally important, they can help you push the envelope on your thinking, learn more about your field though fact-gathering, and connect with other experts.

The publication process for online venues can be easier than for print publications and still provide you with ample carryover flash. The Progressive site Opednews.com, which gets approximately one million unique visitors a month, has a loyal following. The review committee is open-minded and usually responds within a few days. For print publications, even with online components, the editors are more stringent.

If you're aching to get in a specific publication, contact the editor and get information about the publication's submission requirements *before* you send them anything. They're usually willing to provide feedback and help.

The Flash Machine

Public relations (PR), with its news releases, pitch letters, and behind-the-scenes finagling, positions ordinary citizens (and others) as extraordinary experts. This creates a flash response in the audience signaling credibility, notoriety, and trust. Yet, PR is considerably complex. Here are some reasons why:

It's indirect: marketers must create a flash experience in the *editors* that will carry over to the readers. Given journalistic requirements, marketers achieve this by positioning biased marketing content as objective and newsworthy facts.

But some press releases also reach bloggers, customers, the "press" section of their own websites, marketing material, and the public. PR Newswire, a service that sends press releases for clients online, has a distribution that goes right to the public: about 4,000 databases and websites. Depending on the content, the recipients may post the release for a few hours or even a few days.

Releases often contain well-positioned visual components such as sidebars with plenty of white space and, with online venues, flash animation, images, and sound that creates a more robust flash experience. In most cases, though, the primary audience is *not* the end consumer. Rather, it's the media: newspapers, magazines, online news sources, and so on. Thus PR creates indirect flash for the consumer.

Perhaps the most impressive aspect of PR is the amount of flash-triggering language, starting with the headline and reinforced throughout the text. Here is one example:

KING 5: A CASE STUDY

King 5, a Seattle radio show, posted the following release on its website, *www.King5.com*:

Tell us, in 100 words or less, what makes your mom so amazing.

The winning essay will be read LIVE on KING 5 Morning News on KONG 6/16 on Friday, May 9, 2008 between 7 and 9 a.m., as KING 5's Tim Robinson surprises the winning mom and her family at home.

The winning mom receives a night at Hotel Monaco in Seattle, a $100 gift certificate to Sazerac restaurant, and an in-room spa treatment from Relax & Rejuvenate. See the full rules below.

Click here to send an e-mail to mornings@king5.com.

The flash experience developed by the King 5 PR people is all about energy, dare, and excitement. Unlike more traditional types of releases, this one is consistent with the station's voice site and the on-air voices of the DJs.

The release has an embedded brand promise: that the lucky winner will have fifteen minutes of fame. The station will announce the winner on air, probably have banners or fliers, discuss it on the station's website or blog, and have Hotel Monaco, Sazerac, and Relax & Rejuvenate announce it through newsletters, announcements, and their social networks. The announcement doesn't need to *say* any of this: the flash triggers this anticipation.

The strategy does more, though. It builds community and creates buzz, as listeners spread the word and prompt each other to enter. It positions the station as a community member or "friend." Hotel Monaco, Sazerac, and Relax & Rejuvenate benefit from the carryover flash that they glean through the station's efforts to market the contest, as well as their own.

THE ADVERTISING/PR DIFFERENCE

The pitch letter

The pitch letter is similar to the press release because it must engage a media-savvy audience with a compelling message. But, with pitches, marketers hope to get the audience, usually a radio talk show host, television producer, or other media professional, to bring them (or their clients) on the show. The initial flash must be energetic, controversial, shocking, or surprising and most certainly new. On his website, *www.publicityinsider.com*, publicity expert Bill Stoller gives examples of pitch letters, including this one:

December 28, 2008
Mr. Joe Smith
Features Editor
The Daily Herald
Anytown, OH 44444
Dear Joe:

On November 19, during halftime of the California-Stanford game, 80,000 people will make history.

They'll be helping to establish a New World Record by participating in the largest participatory game in—a monumental round of Pictionary, led by the Stanford Marching Band.

The band will use formations to create pictures of words and phrases. The crowd will then have the chance to guess the word, by cheering at the appropriate choice read aloud by the public address announcer.

Rob Angel, the man who began the Pictionary craze, will be in town for the record-setting attempt. In just five years, Rob's risen from waiter to millionaire. One of the most successful game inventors in history, he's now a celebrity in his own right (he was recently featured on the cover of USA Weekend as part of their "Young Millionaires" issue).

Rob will be available to discuss the "Mega-Pictionary" game, and his role as inventor of America's favorite game on Thursday, November 17 or Friday, November 18.

I'll be in touch soon to discuss a possible interview. Look forward to speaking with you.

Sincerely,

Bill Stoller

Media Director

Notice how the flash, about excitement, surprise, and tension—80,000 people making history—is reinforced throughout the letter: the new world record, Rob Angel's history, rising from waiter to millionaire. This should trigger the audience into action. Stoller has an e-newsletter full of tips, which the audience can receive by signing up at his website.

Many publicists pitch through text messaging, which requires a few energetic words and an action statement. For example, Stoller could say: "80,000 people to set new world record with world's most popular game 11–19. When can we talk?" Note the assumptive language of "When can we talk?" He could also employ Twitter, relaying the message in 140 characters.

So far, we've discussed the role of written messages in a public relations campaign. But person-to-person conversations are also important, especially since the success of the pitch could hinge on the marketing person's relationship with the producer.

The conversation itself can function as a sales pitch, in which the marketer finds slices of opportunity to position the offering as something newsworthy and exciting. Here's what a conversation might sound like:

You: Do you think the Widget-Watcher would be good for the morning show?

Producer: Actually I don't think so—we generally focus on family features at that hour.

You: Oh, that's good to know. I'm curious, though, when would you normally feature a product like the Widget Watcher?

Producer: Usually during the afternoon report.

You: Okay, great then. We'd love to have Widget-Watcher on then.

Notice how the interactive discussion creates opportunities that an e-mail, text message, or any other pitch might not. Through conversations like this one, the marketer also gleans information that will help them in future pitches—something lost in electronic venues.

But all articles are most certainly not treated equally and advertisers unquestionably can dictate which stories make the news, which don't, and where they land on the page. This can create an interesting dynamic, especially when marketers position brand representatives as unbiased experts. Sebastian Jones discussed two examples in an article published in *The Nation*. Here's what he said:

President Obama spent most of December 4 touring Allentown, Pennsylvania, meeting with local workers and discussing the economic crisis. A few hours later, the state's former governor, Tom Ridge, was on MSNBC's Hardball With Chris Matthews, offering up his own recovery plan. There were "modest things" the White House might try . . . but the real answer was for the president to "take his green agenda and blow it out of the box." The first step, Ridge explained, was to "create nuclear power plants." Combined with some waste coal and natural gas extraction, you would have an "innovation setter" that would "create jobs, create exports."

As Ridge counseled the administration to "put that package together," he sure seemed like an objective commentator. But what viewers weren't told was that since 2005, Ridge has pocketed $530,659 in executive compensation for serving on the board of Exelon, the nation's largest nuclear power company. As of March 2009, he also held an estimated $248,299 in Exelon stock, according to SEC filings.

Moments earlier, retired general and "NBC Military Analyst" Barry McCaffrey told viewers that the war in Afghanistan would require an additional "three- to ten-year effort" and "a lot of money." Unmentioned was the fact that DynCorp paid McCaffrey $182,309 in 2009 alone. The government had just granted DynCorp a five-year deal worth an estimated $5.9 billion to aid American forces in Afghanistan. The first year is locked in at $644 million, but the additional four options are subject to renewal, contingent on military needs and political realities.

FLASH FOR YOU: The PR prescription
You can get public relations by drafting the releases yourself. If you go online, you'll find dozens of how-to articles about how to get there. Just Google "How

to write a press release" and find whichever works for you. As well, check out *www.prwebdirect.com/pressreleasetips.php* and the online go-to destination, wikihow: *www.wikihow.com/Write-a-Press-Release*. Or go to sites of most medium or large companies (and some small ones) and check their press rooms for ideas. You will need to follow up with the publications to ensure they use the release. From this, you can expect three results:

1. An article that they write about you with an interview. This is ideal.
2. They place your news release in the publication, which is still pretty good.
3. They publish the piece online, in hard copy, or both.

Once the copy is out, be sure to put the release on your site, talk about it to your Facebook or other social network friends, link to it in your blog, and so on. You should also have a "press room" on your website.

Publications: The Dilemma

Flash aside for a moment, the marketing-media relationship can create ethical challenges for article writers. For example, one research group received over a million dollars to determine how workplaces could be safer for workers. They knew that one of the biggest hazards was injuries due to slips and falls. So, they developed an intricate study and spent months executing it. Naturally, their funders expected the researchers to publish papers about the results. Yet, the researchers found the best solution was for employees to keep the floors dry. That's it. Dry floors. How could they position this as a million-dollar finding? They couldn't and, ultimately, merged their findings with a related study. They covered the significance of dry floors to workplace safety and then moved on to sexier subject matter.

Radio Programs

Television and radio are entering new phases of existence, especially as companies create more sophisticated videos and podcasts. Technology has enabled individuals to develop relatively sophisticated productions free from the hermetically sealed atmosphere of the television studio.

Depending on the demographic it's targeting, a less-than-finished production may even have a greater impact than something that comes across as slickly professional. Generation Ys, for example, while heavily marketed to by corporate giants, spend hours watching YouTube videos and other productions, then discussing them with social networking "friends." Ludicrous productions of singing pets and one-person living-room concerts draw the attention of millions of viewers. This proliferation of content has shaped their expectations as well as the flash generated by the media.

Let's focus in on radio. The term "radio" now includes online networks, podcasts, and terrestrial broadcasts that simultaneously air online. This is both an advantage and disadvantage for the radio universe. With all the competition, and the many advertisement-free networks such as NPR and Sirius XM, it's increasingly hard for traditional stations to find means of supporting themselves financially.

Many have resorted to purchasing broadcast content, using DJs only at key hours of the day to maintain a local feel. Others are renting out airtime to business owners and would-be radio personalities who want to get exposure on their own terms. Still others have learned they can purchase a good mike and a modicum of technology at almost any office supply store and create their own podcasts, which run on blogger radio networks, other websites, and radio stations for a fee.

Effectiveness is a different matter. The messaging in the online and on-air universe is dense, and for an amateur (or anyone) to create a message that penetrates it is difficult. Besides, unless the host wants to launch their own career as a media personality, podcasts require an enormous amount of "pull," finding ways to entice the audience to listen in.

Still, radio does give the audience yet another avenue for generating flash—through the voice. According to David Wolf, president of SmallBiz America and a producer at SBTV.com, voice messaging "creates a magic that happens with someone's real voice and their ability to modulate that isn't available in other forms . . . . It reveals the 'who' behind the brand." Today thousands of new voices are entering the marketing universe.

FLASH FOR YOU: So, you want to be a radio star?

Radio shows can have marketing value, but like many other aspects of marketing, they can become their own business. If you're driven because you enjoy doing them, that's great. No question, you can get some marketing value, as well. So, here are your options:

Free radio. These are blogcasts. They're not totally free because you will have to invest in an online blog account and spend lots of time (an expensive resource) organizing guests and creating a worthwhile show.

Pay-per-pod. These AM and FM terrestrial stations host shows, will give you publicity, and produce your interviews . . . for a price. Online networks have been appearing: they're much like Sirius for the talk radio set, with an array of hosts and subject matter from the very-much-aging fitness icon Jack LaLanne to unknowns focused on Hollywood gossip.

Many charge about $2,000 per month, which equals about $500 per show, with the idea that the host will bring in advertisers who will pay for the show—and then some. In theory, this idea is great. But you do have to build a large audience to convince advertisers they should invest their marketing dollars with you.

The Real Deal. Leveraging the traditional mode of broadcasting, you pay the network, which will do the marketing legwork for you and share revenue from advertisers. This is the best possible arrangement, mainly because you get credibility, exposure to an existing network of listeners (as well as benefits from the carryover flash of being on that network), and have an interested party (the network salespeople) taking care of advertising.

In terms of marketing value, radio can provide a decent amount of carryover flash, depending on the network's brand. The difference is clear immediately: CNN versus NPR versus FOX versus Country Rock 101. Even on radio stations with less prestige, it's possible to leverage the host's fame, which can translate into celebrity, expertise, and even leadership.

Soap on Radio

Among the successful hosts of radio programs are some with incredibly narrow niches, such as Donna Maria Coles Johnson, who you met earlier in this book. Her show is the only one dedicated to women with an at-home soap-making business and her numbers have an exceptionally targeted demographic. Advertisers have signed on, which has encouraged Donna Maria to create a social network on her website and sell products to her audience under a revenue-sharing agreement for lucrative results.

Being a guest is another story. To get on-air requires PR: a marketer sends a press release to the stations and follows up with a call to see if it's interested. Most brand representatives don't try to narrow down the show for the sake of carryover flash; most would as easily show up on a tiny station with 500 listeners as NPR. Granted, they'd be happier with NPR, but they'd show up anyway. And why not? Each week, most radio hosts get hundreds of press releases from politicians, musicians, scientists, spies, models, historians, CEOs, and inventors, all trying to sell their brand and themselves.

The Blog Event

Blogs are among the strangest phenomena ever. More than 70,000 new blogs appear every day. A study by BlogHer and Compass Partners found that 35 percent of American women from eighteen to seventy-five enter the blog world once a week. Of women who go online at any time, 53 percent read and 28 percent write or update blogs, while 37 percent post comments.

People read blogs for a variety of reasons. Almost half (46 percent) read blogs primarily for fun; 41 percent to get information; and 34 percent to learn about specific topics.

Bloggers, though largely ordinary citizen journalists or diarists, have amazing credibility. According to a PR Newswire survey, 73 percent of journalists "sometimes" or "always" get information from bloggers, whether content for their stories or insights into public sentiment. Even more, 39 percent use online content in their publication.

Networks within the blogging universe struggle to uphold that credibility. Federated Media Publishing, for example, is a blog network. On its website, the company underscores the credibility of those who blog on its site:

We take our role in the community we serve seriously, and feel responsible for our own words. When we make mistakes, we correct them. We do not seek to use our sites maliciously.

We err on the side of disclosure to our readers. If we have an interest in something we're writing about, we disclose that interest. We are as transparent as we can be about our site's statistics, practices and policies.

Search engines have also enhanced the credibility of blogs, since they frequently have a higher rank for specific subject matter than do online newspapers. According to Andy Wibbels, a blog consultant, search engines like blogs for several reasons. Among them, blogs tend to be newer and fresher than websites, since successful bloggers update their entries at least three times a week.

Blogs tend to be more active than websites, too, with more links coming to and leaving them, which Wibbels says helps page rankings. Also, because HTML technology is, as Wibbels says, "simpler and cleaner," search engines have an easier time indexing and reading them than their website counterparts.

Perhaps the strongest reason for the credibility of blogs is their alleged unbiased approach. Visitors' flash experience of favorite bloggers includes trust and camaraderie. Bloggers' observations, recommendations, and descriptions also trigger enormous amounts of carryover flash.

FLASH FOR YOU: A bit about blogs

Blogs can be a great way to create exposure for your brand and enter online communities. But, the best reason to blog is because you like blogging. These projects demand a considerable amount of attention and focus, and there are better ways of getting marketing attention if your heart isn't in it. Here's what they demand:

Consistency

This is true not only for your blog space in general, but every new entry, including the title, content, visual elements, and sound.

Content

You must have something to say: it should be relevant and meaningful to you as well as the visitor.

Time

Unlike an article, opinion piece, presentation, or even a book, blogs require constant attention; they're never finished. Your blog page must look good, as well as read well, so you must also constantly freshen your visuals.

Audience focus

The audience could be potential customers, voters, other experts who share your views with their colleagues, or the general public. In general, the narrower the demographic, though, the better.

Outcome focus

You must know what you want from your blog. The many possibilities can include online contacts, potential customers, dialogue around issues that interest you, or enhanced credibility.

The Blog-Marketing Connection

Federated Media Publishing understands the importance of blogs in marketing. The company says it is creating an "innovative form of online marketing: a three-way dialog among creators, audiences, and marketers."

The company achieves this by offering brands an opportunity to advertise on popular blogs, usually those having a minimum of 100,000 unique visitors a month. In its sales pitch, Federated Media explains that they have an impressive webpage where they showcase blogs and tracks visitors.

For example, Duct Tape Marketing, with twenty-two bloggers contributing to the site, gets 150,000 visitors a month. Others, such as 43 Folders, a site offering visitors ways to make life easier, get 630,000 page views a month. The site also has stats about the visitors: their age, gender, and other demographics that will interest an advertiser.

One survey showed that 86 percent of bloggers receive pitches from marketers who are increasingly relying on so-called "influencers" or "ambassadors" to spread word about their brand.

To engage them, marketers have launched something akin to a schmooze campaign. They give bloggers free samples, gifts, complimentary tickets, and online previews of events, ostensibly to help them with their reviews. The more popular bloggers may also receive airplane tickets, hotel room stays, invitations to special gatherings, and opportunities to meet and greet with high-level managers. All this encourages bloggers to write about the brand.

Common sense tells us most such reviews will probably be favorable. Why insult a brand who had the good taste to send you a sample to review? Besides, who's going to resist free gifts? As one blogger I interviewed for this book commented, "I get to be the first to try new things and have a voice in how well things go for the brand."

Increasingly marketers are even *paying* bloggers to create a post about their brand. Unlike traditional print media where publishers must state when they receive money and from whom to discuss content, until recently, bloggers didn't have guidelines. According to an article in *Slate*,

> . . . the FTC put bloggers on notice that they could incur an $11,000 fine if they receive free goods, free services, or money and write about the goods or services without conspicuously disclosing their "material connection" to the provider. The FTC guidelines extend even to Facebook and Twitter posters. If you received a gratis novel from the publicity department of a publisher and posted a tweet

about it without disclosing that the book was a freebie, you become an "endorser" in the FTC's view.

Jack Shafer, the author of the *Slate* article, complained (on a page dripping with advertising): "Why is the FTC intent on hounding bloggers?"

Blog: Some Case Studies

Quicken Loans prides itself on being a company that lets people get home mortgage loans quickly. According to the Quicken Loans website, the company knew that it needed a blog but wasn't sure about the best approach. "We just didn't know what to blog about. Mortgages? Finance? Credit? Real Estate? Boring. We really needed to come up with a theme for our blog that could show the things Quicken Loans does best. Then it dawned on us. What makes Quicken Loans special isn't our mortgages. It's our people. It's the things we care about. We call it being the DIFF." The company named its blog "Whatsthediff.com."

In other words, Quicken Loans set out to create a flash experience of trust, comfort, and familiarity at a time when most home loan agencies created flash in the opposite direction. Its tagline read, "Exposing the Gap between Average and Excellent."

The content reinforced that flash with stories and good deeds with a positive slant and a prescriptive nature. In only three weeks, Typepad showcased the blog, calling it "a beautiful new site . . . which takes a unique approach for a corporate blog." WWJ radio in Detroit called it "one of the more innovative corporate blogs."

FLASH FOR YOU: Blog checklist

To make money from blogging means, essentially, creating a second business from your blog. If you are inspired to do so, here's a quick checklist of what you'll need to do:

Create as dynamic a site as possible, with links, videos, and sound.

Provide new information or points and opinions the visitor can get nowhere else.

Avoid talking about what you had for lunch or the event where you took your children unless you can think of a reason why anyone would care.

Invite visitors to comment. Yes, you'll have a comment box, but that won't be enough.

Put a link to your blog on Facebook and anywhere else you can.

Be transparent and let your visitor know when you're writing about products you received free or for pay.

Comments, Anyone?

Comments are an unusual twist on the opinion page or letters to the editor. Comments can help bloggers improve their search engine ranking, generate buzz, and help them gauge their audience's take on the content. As a marketing tool, comments can create some carryover flash largely because of the "principle of social acceptance" which we'll discuss in the next chapter.

Consumers like brands that other consumers like, too—that are socially acceptable to their peers. Hence, phrases such as "The most popular . . ." "Number 1 in our industry . . ." "A leading brand . . ." and "The fastest growing . . ." register with audiences. For years, McDonald's posted the number of hamburgers sold on their street signs. In 1963, that number was 1 million. In 1975 it was 5 billion, according to the company history.

Today, according to an NBC news report, "McDonald's estimates 550 million Big Macs are sold each year in the United States alone. Do the math and that's about 17 per second . . ." making a numbers count ludicrous, obviously. Its' also difficult to determine and update. Instead, the signs say "Billions and Billions Served" or something related to that theme. In essence, the idea of social acceptance comes down to this: "Billions and billions of people can't be wrong."

When a blog has lots of comments, the flash is one of importance, acceptance, even credibility. Those numbers can vary, depending on the blog: some get as few as one or two in a year, while others may have tens of thousands.

The tone of the comments can also affect the carryover flash. On a basic level, the language itself can create a sense of ease, belonging, and community independent of the content. For example, in the gamer blog joystiq.com, Griffen McElroy wrote his blog called "Dragon Age: Journeys Bonus Items Transfer to Origins." Notice the comments on the blog, this one from Freak Mojo:

> Okay . . . count me in. This is pretty cool tie-in . . . even if it is more of a time-suck. Hopefully, I can get into the web game here at work :P

The community is built organically: the comments come from those who are engaged in the conversation. Now, notice the difference in the following company blog from "Essential U," the site of Essential Wholesale.com, makers of natural and organic soaps, cleaners, and aromas. Their demographic is women, among them stay-at-home moms with home-based businesses. One blog entry featured an interview with Ken and Amber Harper, who started a home-based soap and fragrance business. Here are a few of the comments:

> Great interview! The average American watches 4.5 hours of tv per day and that's the amount of time it would take to start a small business. What a great example of that. Thank you for the interview; it's inspiring to see what happens when you work on something with a shared purpose and common values.

And this one from Ken's daughter:

> Dad, you make me so proud! I really do look up to you guys and love you alot!

Notice the words "shared" and "common" in the first comment and "proud" and "love" in the next. The language triggers carryover flash of warmth, kindness, empathy, safety, and other feelings that are deeply meaningful to this audience. This can have a carryover effect on the products themselves, endorsed by like-minded people. Ken's daughter's heartfelt expression also speaks to Ken's homemade goods. Would a guy like that sell anything but the best?

Marketers obviously value positive and well-positioned comments. Professional agencies encourage their consultants to write blogs and solicit positive comments from friends, colleagues and anyone else who's willing. Adam Cahill works for the agency Hill Holiday. His blog is located on the company site and on ClickZ, a site for digital insiders. His blog dated February, 10, 2010, wins comments that open with this one:

Mr. Cahill makes many excellent points, but none more relevant than the mixing it up with the competition. This not only gives an impression of relevance, but IS momentum itself . . . .

His blog dated January 14, 2010, "Catching up to Mobile," won comments that started with the following:

Great points Adam

Adam,
This is the day. This is the hour. I fully agree.

Spot on Adam. I've been following this trending for our company, TETCO, which is a retail convenience store chain.

These brief odes to Cahill's insights may or may not be sincere. But it's no secret that professionals, from authors to researchers, encourage colleagues and friends to comment positively—if not effusively. Whether the comments create carryover flash may depend on the way the comment is worded. A sincere-sounding comment will certainly register in a different way from an insincere or forced one.

Active comments also serve another function: to boost the search engine ranking. ClickZ, in the interests of creating true communities, cautions against this on its "About Us" section: "We do monitor comments. We discourage and will remove comments . . . that contribute little to the conversation other than to [lift] the poster's search rankings."

In a larger sense, phony comments can dampen the flash carryover effect. If a visitor suspects that comments in general are rigged, then he'll surely suspect the comments in particular.

AS FOR BOOKS . . .

Books are the perfect venue for those with a burning desire to discuss issues of consequence. For those primarily hoping for marketing attention, though, books can be a costly way of getting it. Many others are involved in the book-making process, including editors, agents, and distributors, and they get a cut of the profits. And, for the amount of time authors need to write the book, which can be a year or longer, the hourly fee is negligible.

Once the book is out, the authors must invest time and energy into marketing them. The publishing industry has shrunk its publicity budgets to peanut size. Some still have in-house publicists, but many don't. The authors' job is to fill the gap, sending news releases, contacting media, and selling their books at talks, conferences, and everywhere else.

This entails another curve, though: authors must market themselves to publishers. Got that? Authors must market the marketing effort that will ultimately market their marketing. If you're not clear, don't worry. Just keep reading.

Two components of a book proposal are critical for publishers: a great book idea and a platform through which the author is well known, well positioned, and knowledgeable enough to appeal to potential readers.

Publishers rarely speak with authors directly—at least in the deal-making stages of a book—but rather to agents who, some reports indicate, are harder for authors to obtain than book deals. So, aspiring authors must market themselves to agents, who market them to the publisher, which publishes the book, which the author markets to the public, so consumers will read (or at least purchase) it.

Recognizing this, plenty of authors self-publish. Self-published books rarely find their way to bookstores and get lost in sites such as Amazon. Even more, the flash experience created by such a book may not be a positive one since self-published books don't have the polish or panache of those published by commercial houses. In other words, the book may look cheap and amateurish.

Of course, books *can* have significant marketing value. Many have launched entire careers *and* methodologies, health programs, and product lines with them. Tom Peters, for example, a former Navy man and drug abuse advisor for the Nixon White House, set fire to his career in 1982, when he published his book *In Search of Excellence*. He gained national exposure through a PBS broadcast of television specials based on the book, which Peters hosted.

Another famous example is the Chicken Soup for the Soul series. Authors and motivational speakers Jack Canfield and Mark Victor Hansen endured numerous rejections before their book, a collection of inspirational stories, was published. The Chicken Soup for the Soul website tells us:

> We have been helping real people share real stories for fifteen years, bringing hope, courage, inspiration and love to hundreds of millions of people around the world . . . .

Get it? Hundreds of millions. New books include *Chicken Soup for the Soul True Love*. Okay, we expect that, but how about this improbable addition: *Chicken Soup for the Soul NASCAR*.

The book series inspired a product line including clothing, Bibles (seriously), cards, and through the wonders of brand extension, Chicken Soup for the Pet Lover's Soul: "wholesome" foods for dogs and cats. The brand has even launched an effort to fight pet obesity.

Collections of other people's stories are as old as the Bible and not necessarily an interesting concept. Most likely, the Chicken

Soup for the Soul series can attribute much of its success to the flash experience of trust, love, nurturing, mothering, and goodness generated by the title. Like everything about the series, how Canfield and Hansen developed the title was unusual. No focus groups, brainstorming sessions, or committee meetings at the publishers. Here's what the website tells us:

> As they searched for a winning title, Jack & Mark each agreed to meditate on the subject for one hour a day. Jack visualized the image of his grandmother's chicken soup and remembered how she told him it would cure anything. The book would have the same healing powers as that soup, but not for the body—for the soul. Thus, the now famous title was born . . . Chicken Soup for the Soul.

CHAPTER 7:

Flash! Review

Articles can help enhance your credibility but probably won't generate business or intense marketing exposure.

Publishing articles online can be easier, with a faster review process, than hard copy and reach a large audience.

PR can generate some interesting rewards, but your message must have tension and newness for it to make a splash.

Most news evolves from press releases. You can develop one yourself or hire a specialist to draft it for you.

You must give the audience something that other bloggers can't.

Blogs can fuel your marketing efforts, but you must be specific about how.

If you think you don't have time for a blog, don't worry. Plenty of successful brands don't have them. If you do want one, do it with enthusiasm and commitment.

Image means much to generating sustainable flash, so be sure to add photos, links, videos, and other images.

You will need to market your blog, if people are to read it. Even links can help.

Depending on how controversial the blog, you may need a game plan, or at least psychological stamina, to contend with negative press.

8. Let's Get Social

The concept of marketing within communities is hardly new: that was the underpinning of marketing before it existed as a separate discipline. We have always lived together in communities that offer us protection and more or less ensure that we meet our fundamental needs of food, clothing, shelter, and procreation. Throughout time, even marriage was a brokered commodity dictated by social standing, commerce, and traditions.

Modern marketing is interesting in that respect. Our efforts are geared toward providing services and products we don't actually need, from online video games to overseas vacations. Yet, for marketers to succeed in their campaigns, they must tap those same impulses that once ensured our survival.

Playing to Our Needs

One of these needs, according to Abraham Maslow, is love and belonging, which are associated in turn with family, friends, and sexual intimacy. Those themes play out in countless marketing campaigns.

Consider, for example, AT&T's classic campaign tagline: "Reach out and touch someone." Certainly no one needs a telephone for survival and through most of human history we've lived without them. But we do need community, friends and family, to help ensure our survival.

The tagline works incredibly well on numerous levels. For one, it has a strong physical component centered around the words "reach," "out," and "touch." You can feel the motion of reaching and the physicality built into the metaphor "touch," as opposed to a statement like "Call someone you haven't heard from in a while." The tagline also creates a flash experience of fear, yearning, even loneliness: if you must reach out, then you are far from the comfort zone of your community.

In his classic book *Influence: The Psychology of Persuasion*, Robert Cialdini discusses how marketing also triggers impulses woven into our societal contracts, whether we're aware of them or not. Here are some of them:

RECIPROCITY

This concept is endemic to our social interactions. A friend buys you lunch at work. The next time you go out for lunch, you pick up the tab. You take your neighbor's kid on an outing and within a week or two your friend will take yours. Cialdini says that at one time, when someone handed you a gift or did you a favor, you would say, "Much obliged." That phrase of acknowledgment has since become "Thank you," but the reality of being obligated or obliged prevails.

In social networks, reciprocity is demonstrated constantly. When a company sends bloggers a sample, the expectation is that they'll write about it. When a social network gets information before setting up an account, the audience knows that the network is using it for a variety of purposes, including targeting their own marketing or selling the information to others. But the audience provides the information in return for the benefits they gain from joining the network.

Marketers constantly create a flash experience that wins reciprocity. With free samples, for example, marketers increase the chances the customer will buy something, if not that particular product. Home Depot offers free workshops at the store, knowing the audience will buy supplies from them afterward. The feeling of reciprocity is so deeply engrained that the audience will do so *unthinkingly* even if the same supplies are available for half price at Lowe's two doors down.

BELONGING

A sense of belonging is central to our existence as a species. We forge tribes, cliques, and clubs that define us and are instrumental to our survival. In the online universe, these clubs go by the names of Facebook, MySpace, LinkedIn, and countless other smaller social networks. They have membership, which may be based on self-selection or "invitation" by "friends." The "friends" speak the same language (effectively, geek-speak), and discuss specific interests, which creates an insular quality that, for better or worse, engenders a flash experience of trust.

The intensity and marketing promise of belonging is played out in the direct marketing universe of Mary Kay, Avon, Tupperware, and countless other "living room marketers." They owe the loyalty of their "sales force" (largely unsalaried, commission-based "entrepreneurs") to a sense of belonging. Here's how the Mary Kay website says it:

With Mary Kay, you thrive as part of an international sisterhood—now 900,000 strong, committed to Mary Kay's mission to enrich

*women's lives. Where your work is more than a business or a paycheck.
It's a passion and a lifestyle . . . .*

The number of other marketing campaigns that tap the audience's need to belong is limitless. One of the most common is the supermarket "club" cards in which the audience must apply for membership. The flash of belonging gets triggered every time the consumer presents his card and gets a discount on his purchases. The irony, of course, is that no one is denied this "membership." They simply sign up.

FLASH FOR YOU: Belong to me?

You don't have to turn your entire company into a members-only enterprise. Some businesses offer a "10 percent club," for example, in which members who regularly spend a certain amount get 10 percent off. A small bookstore I know has a "kids club" that offers discounts and special programs for kids who frequent the store. Regardless, you must have a strong brand identity for your club. Are you appealing to a hip audience? Upscale? Smart? You need to articulate this in all of your documentation, including your club cards, e-mail updates, and website.

EXCLUSIVITY

The concept of exclusivity has propelled people to buy brands. Fine clothing stores have by-invitation openings on new lines, exclusively for their members. Auto insurance companies have special discounts for members of their "safe driving clubs," as opposed to less-compelling fee structures built into the contract.

A moment ago we discussed supermarket membership cards. Exclusivity also plays a part of their undying popularity: while other people, those non-community members, pay full price, the audience gets huge discounts. In some stores, the cashier even says things like, "Congratulations, you saved $20," or something similar.

SOCIAL ACCEPTANCE

We discussed "social acceptance" when addressing the comments section of social networks and websites. Direct marketing plays off this concept incredibly well. I once attended a marketing "party" thrown by a friend whose niece was the salesperson. As her niece espoused the virtues of the creams and exfoliates, the other guests (many of them relatives) made comments like: "I've used that and I love it." In spite of myself, I purchased a bottle of wrinkle cream (which, I may add, is still sitting unused in my medicine cabinet). It's worth noting that reciprocity also played a role: at these events the direct sales marketers ply you with chocolate, wine, and other treats that more or less demand a response.

Marketers also tap social acceptance through testimonials, quotes from happy customers, case studies, and before-and-after samples.

American Express

American Express has embraced the membership strategy, even dropping its advertising campaign, "My life. My card." in favor of "Are you a cardmember?" The intention is for the audience to believe they're more than holders of a credit card, but members of an exclusive club.

As a *New York Times* article points out, the company uses card "member" in place of the traditional card "holder." "Now, we want to go into more depth about what you get out of membership," Diego Scotti, American Express global head of marketing, said about the shift in strategy. "What has changed is the stories will be connected to product, in an authentic way." In other words, the company is triggering the audience's impulse for social acceptance, particularly useful at a time when public distrust of financial institutions is at an all-time high.

If you go to the American Express homepage, *www.americanexpress .com*, the play on "membership" is impressive. It repeats consistently, reinforcing the flash experience. In one corner, a link reads: "Members since 1958. Meet some of our original card members." This reinforces the flash experience of belonging to a true club, whose members joined at different times. Once someone clicks on the box, they realize just how important that club really is. Or, as the header reads: "We are celebrating the extraordinary lives of cardmembers who have been with us from the start."

These include an Olympic athlete, a U.S. senator, a female stock car racer, and a professor of biomedical engineering. Amex also has the "preferred" membership, which isn't exactly novel; virtually every insurance and financial corporation has them. American Express, however, promises an exclusivity that is well over the top: "A special class of membership." Members within the membership.

FLASH FOR YOU: A good read

Robert Cialdini's book *Influence: The Psychology of Persuasion*, which we discussed earlier, provides amazing information about why and how people make their purchasing decisions—and plenty more. It can help you develop your marketing strategy and even give you insights into yourself. It's a quick, easy read—good for airplane reading, too.

Social Networks: Beyond Flash

Online social networking has been the rage in the marketing universe for almost a decade.

The options for social networking are impressive: go to Wikipedia and you'll find a list of about fifty of the most popular social networking venues—ranging from thousands to millions of community members.

According to marketer Michael Selzner, the top ones on the list are Twitter, blogs, LinkedIn, Facebook, YouTube and other videos, social bookmarking sites, and forums. These communities are relatively new—some a mere few years old.

TWITTER

Twitter is a micro-blogging platform, meaning you send short messages of 140 characters, to the audience. You can invite people to "follow" you, or you can follow them. Tweets are bits of (hopefully interesting) conversation that get scattered into the universe, eventually creating a meaningful trail. Barack Obama, for example, used Twitter to update his followers on the campaign trail. JetBlue, like many brands, uses it to promote special offers. For small businesses, who have a more personal attachment to their customers, Twitter offers one way to create a sense of belonging and exclusivity: they tweet their followers about special offers, contests, or events not open to the public.

FACEBOOK

The site, launched in 2004, was originally for Harvard students only. A lot has changed since then and now practically everyone joins. Facebook has over 400 million active users with the largest growth area in the over-twenty-five demographic. In fact, many in the blogosphere have speculated that Facebook is becoming the nest for "geezers." Facebook also has an aggressive translation program and twenty versions of the site in languages other than English, including one in Chinese.

LINKEDIN

LinkedIn is a social networking site for businesspeople hoping to make connections. I've received more invitations to become a "friend" than I can count. Interestingly, all the invitations came from colleagues in the forty-plus age range.

MYSPACE

This network, launched in 2003, has attracted the younger, more social (as opposed to businesslike) crowd. It was once perceived as a bastion for high school students (although 85 percent of American users are eighteen and over) and has an informal nature.

Some in the social networking community think that MySpace is on the way out. But according to one *New York Times* article, it's simply going through identity changes. Even the jewelry company Cartier has launched a MySpace page to encourage Cartier-type members. MySpace acts as a bouncer determining who will get through the virtual doors to make the company's "friends" list and who won't. Are you a gun-slingin', dope-tokin' kind of friend? Better go elsewhere.

SHORT-TERM COMMUNITIES

Some online communities exist for specific reasons and are, by nature, short term. For example, Starbucks wanted to engage customers, so it created a website called My Starbucks Idea. There it invited customers to give ideas about what they wanted from the company. The feedback ranged from stoppers in the hole in the lid of the coffee cup to keep the coffee from sloshing out, to mugs that were suitable for left-handed people. In many cases, Starbucks employees commented on the ideas, as did lots of other customers. You can review the site at *www.mystarbucksidea.com.*

NICHE COMMUNITIES

Perhaps the best social communities for marketers are the smaller, acutely focused ones. While Facebook and other larger networks have "fan clubs" and discussion boards, smaller networks are more focused and personal. In many cases, the friends personally know the brand or individual hosting the network.

For example, SBTV, an online multimedia forum that includes streams and television for small businesses, also has a social network. One of the partners, Susan Solovic, is an author and travels widely to give talks and promote issues affecting small business owners, including women. This demographic, many of whom know Solovic personally, finds a small enough community, with clearly targeted content, to make their engagement worthwhile.

FLASH FOR YOU: Love 'em and leave 'em. It's all right.
The beauty of belonging to a social network is that it doesn't cost much; you'll get invited to become friends pretty quickly, and, unlike a blog, if you don't show up for months at a time, no one will care. If you find social networks boring, just move onto something else.

Then There's YouTube

If not precisely a marketing opportunity, YouTube is a chance to dive into the online culture. The site, while a mere three years old as of this writing, has created a virtual labyrinth of video possibilities. According to its website, YouTube has "attracted users at a meteoric rate [and] has 71 million unique users each month and has the 6th largest audience on the Internet." In fact, the site tells us, 75 percent of Americans watched a video online last month.

According to the stats, from its online "videocracy" YouTube reaches a vast demographic throughout the United States. A full 69 percent have been to college. They're dedicated, too: more than half go to the site every week or more, and 50 percent say they watch the videos to the end.

FLASH FOR YOU: You—tube?

Most likely, you know about the inner workings of YouTube. If not, here's what happens: you can upload a video to the site at no cost. The video can be about you, your business, or virtually anything else that interests you, with some exceptions. Porn is out. Violence is out. Defaming individuals—also out. You can post other people's videos with their permission.

You can put your broadcast on your website, but gaining exposure directly from YouTube requires a heavy amount of work—once you're up there, how can anyone find you? You need to let your audience know through announcements, links, and even press releases—online or otherwise.

If you want to maximize your exposure, YouTube offers you plenty of opportunities to advertise. For a fee, the site will position your video so the audience is likely to see it, whether on the site's homepage of featured videos or first in its lineup for specific searches. You can also have a short—roughly fifteen-second—film, before or after the YouTube entry.

The Business Side of Being Social

Since the 2008 election campaign, the value of social marketing has become clearer, although not totally transparent. In one study of 900 marketing professionals, Michael Selzner found that the social networks brought these rewards:

- Generated exposure for the business: 81%
- Increased traffic/subscriber/opt-in list: 61%
- Resulted in new business partnerships: 56%
- Helped us rise in the search engines: 52%
- Generated qualified leads: 48%
- Reduced my overall marketing expenses: 45%
- Helped me close business: 35%

You'll notice that the top result is not that social networks help brands *close* business. That makes sense, given that social networks really are about building relationships. The flash experience that we've talked about in this book may be restricted by the short form of most social networking communications. More likely, though, the social networking universe frowns on overt marketing overtures. The strong and often creative language that triggers a flash experience gets watered down to a "conversation" between acquaintances.

Like most relationships, social ones build slowly. The quick, energized tone and the metaphors that trigger so many associations appear cheesy, much as a sale representative pitching his brand at a family wedding. The social network also demands time. According to Selzner,

A significant 64 percent of marketers are using social media for 5 hours or more each week and 39 percent for 10 or more hours

weekly. It is interesting to note that 9.6 percent spend more than 20 hours each week with social media.

He added that employees are twice as likely as business owners to commit 20+ hours a week to social media.

The results of social networking take time to realize, as well. Thus the irony of the high-speed, fast-paced social networking age is that results come slowly. According to marketing blogger Lee Odden:

> *There's both a social/play and a social/communicate aspect to Twitter that makes it productive as a promotional tool for pointing to interesting things you've found on the web as well as a tool for building credibility and influence. On their own, such updates can be blasé and uninteresting. However, followed over time, you can gain insight into people you may end up hiring, getting hired by, working for, partnering with or simply socializing with.*

The Social Networking Beat

In an interview on NPR's *Marketplace Morning Report*, Billboard's Bill Werde explains that musicians have generated plenty of meaningful buzz.

> *. . . A lot of these artists are recognizing that the fan expectation has changed in terms of interacting with the artist, and so you'll see artists sort of commenting on fan pages, commenting on fan blogs . . . 160,000 fans of 50 Cent . . . have created an account on www.ThisIs50.com, that's 160,000 fans that 50 Cent has an e-mail*

address for, maybe even has a cell phone number for. In the context of the music business, that's incredibly valuable information.

Werde added that the artists own the space and can sell advertising on it—an additional benefit for really successful social networkers.

USING THE SOCIAL NETWORK TO GENERATE SALES

Coming into the social network universe, marketers are entering a newly formed sphere of transparency with its own codes of conduct. For example, marketers shouldn't promote their brands, but users can discuss them. Marketers should never pose as users, and users should acknowledge whether they work for the company that produces the product they're discussing. This creates a problem for marketers. How do they promote a product in a setting that condemns promotion?

Many find surrogates—so-called brand ambassadors—to speak for them. Others cheat. Be forewarned that the online universe can be attuned to these wrongdoings, and spread the word quickly.

Outed in New Zealand . . . And Everywhere Else

The New Zealand company Ferrit, an online mall website, touted its $325 Dualit toaster on Spareroom.com by masquerading as a blogger. Here's what one of the pseudo-bloggers said: "Yeah it's a little spendy for a toaster but if you love cool appliances that work brilliantly a Dualit is worth getting. I love the fact that you can determine exactly how brown you want your toast using the timer."

Bloggers saw through the scam and outed Ferrit.

Other outed bloggers include Steve Jobs and Al Gore. Even Amazon.com is crosschecking books with glowing, five-star reviews that feature a writing style sharply resembling that of the author.

THE NATIONAL BOOK EXPO

It *is* possible for your giveaway to be like everyone else's and still be effective. Take Book Expo, the annual meet-up place for publishers, bookstore owners, book dealers, and others in the industry. The exhibition hall is crammed with booths and the prerequisite giveaways—pens, squeeze balls, candy, and the like. (Publishers may be smarter, or at least better readers than the rest of us, but that doesn't mean they have marketing sense.)

Only one publisher, whose name I won't mention in this book (Okay, okay, McGraw-Hill), had something different. A bag. People literally lined up at the publisher's booth to get one, which was a noteworthy feat in a conference practically chock-full of famous authors—not to mention businesspeople, movie stars, and cartoonists—signing their most recent books. In fact, the longest line (actually the longest *unmoving* line, since the giveaway of the giveaways hadn't started) was for the bags.

The plot thickens because our crafty (or frugal) publisher didn't have enough bags for all the conference attendees. So, they posted a sign explaining that the bags were only for those who sold or helped in the selling of books.

This strategy (which may not have actually been a strategy) was ingenious. Here's why:

- **Relationship building:** The bags lured people to the booth, where young, smart, and well-coiffed editors eagerly awaited them.

- **Scarcity:** The limited quantity created enhanced value—that scarcity marketing strategy I told you about earlier.
- **Exclusivity:** These bags were for the chosen few . . . the flattered (and lucky) customer.
- **Buzz:** People asked where the McGraw-Hill booth was so they could try their luck at getting a bag—where they were greeted by young, attractive salespeople, and editors waiting to discuss their latest publications.

And Speaking of Influencers

According to Bill Bishop, author of *The Big Sort*, communities are increasingly homogeneous, making it easier for marketers to target their message. For example, Bishop says Democrats favor more compact living environments, while Republicans like space. Typically Democrats are less likely to use pesticides, and Republicans more so. These commonalities exist at many levels, from the news broadcasts they watch (Republicans watch Fox and Democrats MSNBC) to their views on family and lifestyle issues.

This presents a considerable number of opportunities for marketers: by tapping distinct, closely knit communities in neighborhoods, towns, and cities, a brand can rapidly penetrate the culture. Enter "word of mouth" marketing. With this popular, yet obvious, marketing strategy, people talk about the brand, spreading the word themselves.

The underpinning of word of mouth, according to Emanuel Rosen, author of *The Anatomy of Buzz*, is that we like, and need, to talk. He says, "Sharing information is an effective survival mechanism for ravens, bees, ants . . . and people. We may no longer need to trade information about bison hunting, but we're still programmed to do so." Besides, it helps us to make better choices in the cluttered marketplace.

As "word of mouth" suggests, the flash experience for the audience is through carryover. An overly embellished message can smack of disingenuous intent. Yet, a too-casual one will go unnoticed. For that reason, most word-of mouth campaigns straddle the line, often relying on the honest opinions of individuals and at other times creating hype so people will want to spread the word for them.

FLASH FOR YOU: Grass and not-fors

If you are a marketer engaged in not-for-profits and political and social activist campaigns, then word of mouth can be a great advantage to you. People are eager to spread ideas and information that better their communities. The price is right, and many of the venues for spreading the word, such as fairs, town meetings, community sections of newspapers, and online communities are already in place and predisposed to hear your message.

The Word of Mouth Marketing Association breaks their marketing strategy into two categories on its website: *www.womma.org/wom101/wom101.pdf.*

Organic word of mouth occurs when people become advocates because they are happy with a product and have a natural desire to share their support and enthusiasm. Practices that enhance organic word of mouth activity include:

Focusing on customer satisfaction
Improving product quality and usability
Responding to concerns and criticism
Opening a dialog and listening to people
Earning customer loyalty

Amplified word of mouth occurs when marketers launch campaigns designed to encourage or accelerate word of mouth in existing or new communities. Practices that amplify word of mouth activity include:

Creating communities
Developing tools that enable people to share their opinions
Motivating advocates and evangelists to actively promote a product
Giving advocates information that they can share
Using advertising or publicity designed to create buzz or start a conversation
Identifying and reaching out to influential individuals and communities
Researching and tracking online conversations.

Organic word of mouth generally has a more relaxed (and slower) flow of information, where people have "conversations" and "discuss" matters rather than rant about them. The flash experience tends to be muted since it's based on carryover flash and entails more cognitive processing than does a highly energized message. It's possible that organic word of mouth is more realistic and sincere because it's slower; the realities of the brand, or discord about it, have more time to seep in and shape the discussion.

Amplified word of mouth is all about energy: the language, images, and strategies, including the much-touted buzz, are oriented to give the audience a charge. The difference between amplified word of mouth and straight advertising is that amplified word of mouth still relies on third parties to ignite discussion. The carryover flash is usually more intense, as marketers often put time limits, challenges, and other forms of motivation into the campaign. The list can include contests, outrageous stunts, daring advertising gimmicks, challenges, and more.

Word of mouth can occur through a campaign that generates excitement throughout the general population. Or marketers may strategically target influential individuals within specific communities who will spread the word about their brand.

These influencers can include bloggers, as we discussed earlier; political figures; community leaders; less obvious personalities such as popular high school students or parents actively engaged in their children's schools; and famous people.

For example, every time a race for a Senate seat is close, the president or some other high-powered figure will rush in to rally support for his candidate. Marie Osmond came out of career hibernation to be a spokesperson for the Nutrisystem diet plan. The flash associated with the famous person transfers to the brand.

FLASH FOR YOU: Influencer hub

To find the influencers in your community, check out these places:

- Visitors and Tourist Bureaus
- Newspapers (online and hard copy) for local columnists
- Religious institutions, especially those with community programs
- Businesses with an emphasis on service to your demographic
- Leaders in networking groups
- Individuals in charge of community listservers
- People involved in the arts, such as heads of arts collectives

Babies, Breasts, and Anger Management

The Massachusetts-based company iParty, true to its name, sells party goods, including birthday party supplies for the kids. So—no surprise—plenty of mothers, some with nursing babes, show up at their fifty stores to make their purchases.

All was well until one day a mother was nursing her baby on the floor of one of the iParty stores, just outside the receiving door. According to Denell Nuese, iParty's director of marketing, pallets loaded with supplies constantly went through that door and the manager was afraid the mother and child would get hurt. He asked the mother to relocate somewhere else in the store. He also stepped into a public relations snafu: he made the request at a time when legislation about breastfeeding was pending in Massachusetts—one of the few states not to have a law on the subject—and tempers were running high on the subject.

The nursing mom was offended, believing the iParty manager was infringing on her nursing rights. She contacted the local media and the fast-acting blogging community, who ran with the subject. Soon, so-called lactivists were calling for a "nurse out" in front of the store and a boycott. Remember—this is a company where moms are the coveted customer.

"We started going online to reason with the bloggers who were talking about it," Nuese said, but they were unyielding. "We were shocked—we just couldn't stop the moving train." Nuese added that twenty years ago the word wouldn't have spread so quickly, reaching so many people at one time, with so many interpretations. She added the flipside: "If this were twenty years ago, we would have been faxing back and forth and wouldn't have understood the magnitude of the situation. Because people post online, though, we could see what they were planning and could control it."

So, Nuese went on the offensive and targeted influencers, among them the most vocal woman in the nurse-out. She said that iParty would train male employees to handle the matter differently in the future. The company brought in other influencers, as well, including the Boston Medical Center (the iParty chairman had a long relationship with the center and had even launched the breastfeeding clinic there), who contacted bloggers and others online saying that the iParty folks were okay. Meanwhile, Nuese invited the lactivists to turn their "nurse out" into a "nurse in"—a nursing extravaganza inside the store complete with refreshments, balloons, and coloring books for the kids.

The event brought lots of positive publicity, and iParty was featured on numerous websites, blogs, and old-fashioned media. iParty's success was due to carryover flash from the influencers, and a flash experience of fun and belonging at the nurse-in that would create a flash memory strong enough to endure.

Seeds, Anyone?

"Seeding" occurs when marketers get samples of their brands to core demographics, usually through a number of venues from street teams who give the product away outside subway stations or other crowded areas to supermarkets who offer them to their shoppers.

One example that Rosen describes in his book is the launch of the game Trivial Pursuit in 1984. As one of its strategies, the game's publisher had over a hundred radio stations broadcast trivia questions on the air and gave away games to listeners. This was a great way to engage the listeners, give them an experience of the brand (and create ownership), and ignite word of mouth.

It's important to recognize, though, that the flash response for the listener carried over from the radio; it was all about fun, pleasure, excitement, and belonging. The listener identified with whatever type of music was broadcast on the station, and the demographic who listened to it. This identification is deep, encompassing politics, age, ethnicity, lifestyle, and marital status, all carried over to a tantalizing and thought-provoking game. Even the DJs' voices reinforced that flash. Imagine the difference if a nurse at a clinic asked patients those questions to distract them while they waited for surgery. Or if teachers played the game with their students. The flash experience wouldn't be the same.

The influence of word-of-mouth marketing, including bloggers, may be petering out, though. According to the Word of Mouth Marketing Association:

After a year of brands desperately infiltrating the social space, the consumers have issued backlash. The number of people who feel their friends are credible sources of information about a company dropped from 45 percent in 2008 to 25 percent today. Before dumping your WOM [word of mouth] stock, know that TV news, radio news and newspapers also saw significant drops in trust. It turns out the general public is becoming a fairly distrustful group. WOM marketing relies on the value people put on the opinions of others. In pursuit of more impressions, a saturation point may have been reached. Impressions are significant only when they are made with the right people. To reach them, consider making the opt-in a high priority in any campaign.

BUZZ MARKETING, WOM, AND OTHER CHATTER

Buzz marketing is an amplified, marketer-driven approach that essentially shocks the audience into talking. The flash experience is usually about energy, wonder, excitement, confusion, sexiness, and even outrage. This accelerates the speed at which the message spreads and can create faster sales for the brand. What's most amazing is that the buzz campaigns may only have a slight connection to the purpose of the brand.

Let's look in more detail at two examples that we addressed briefly earlier in the book.

Half.com

Half.com is a lot like eBay (in fact, it was bought by eBay). Customers bid on products, primarily books, videos, music, and movies . . . but not of the antique, quirky, and used variety that you associate with eBay. They're more of a button-down operation with online edge. However, Half.com launched two edgy, risky, and daring campaigns in order to generate buzz. The strategy worked so well the marketing effort garnered attention in the *Wall Street Journal* and on *60 Minutes*.

For the first strategy, the company's marketing VP, Mark Hughes, convinced the town of Halfway, in Oregon near the Idaho border, to change its name to Half.com—the name of the company—for one year. The town agreed for a price of $100,000 and twenty computers. The strategy won Half.com enormous publicity, focusing *not* on the website but on the name change.

Hughes also came up with the second idea: to put the company's name on urinal screens, the plastics gizmos in urinals that keep gum or cigarette butts—or who knows what—from clogging the pipes. The price was right—each screen cost $1.34—and unquestionably the venue was original. They put the name on the screens and the tagline: "Don't Piss Away Your Money. Head to Half.com."

Obviously the ideas, especially the urinal, were risky. But risk is a requirement of buzz campaigns. How else can marketers cut through the so-called "noise" of messaging to reach the audience?

In this case, Mark Hughes said the campaign was a success: "We braced ourselves for the reaction . . . friends and family members called us laughing from their cell phones leaving us messages to the effect: 'You'll never guess what I saw!' Everyone called. Everyone e-mailed. Most were amazed and most congratulated us for 'boldly going where no brand has gone before.'"

Cartoon Network goes haywire

Cartoon Network's marketing campaign was headed by creative agency Interference, Inc., which intended to generate buzz for its client's upcoming movie, *Aqua Teen Hunger Force*. So the agency created electronic devices about half the size of a baking pan, with a robot-looking figure giving the finger to passersby in Boston, New York City, Los Angeles, Chicago, Atlanta, Seattle, Portland, Austin, San Francisco, and Philadelphia. They attached these figures to spots throughout the cities, including the sides of bridges, with *no* indication of what they were.

They intended to create an unresolved flash experience (surprise, excitement, and curiosity) that would generate buzz and prolong the audience's experience to make it memorable. Unfortunately, the flash response in Boston was fear from residents who thought the boxes were bombs. The two employees who planted the marketing gimmicks, Sean Stevens and Peter Berdovsky, were arrested for "placing a hoax device" and disorderly conduct.

The fallout was more than embarrassing. Protesters gathered outside the Charlestown court where Stevens and Berdovsky appeared for the hearing, insisting that Turner Broadcast Systems, which owns Cartoon Network, take full responsibility. The charges against the two employees were ultimately dropped—although both had to provide community service, and Turner Broadcast Systems and Interference, Inc., the agency behind the campaign, had to pay a total of $2 million.

Cluck-Cluck Buzz

Some negative buzz can hurt the brand, like the negative buzz about Microsoft's Vista, John Edwards's twisted love life, and Arthur Andersen's poor judgment in the Enron case. Politicians use negative buzz about issues ranging from abortion to gay marriage, not to convince the opposition but to rally constituents to their cause. People for the Ethical Treatment of Animals (PETA) has mastered the art of rallying sympathizers and convincing outliers to boycott brands, call Congressional representatives, and take direct actions against those, for instance, who wear fur. Such tactics have garnered the group negative buzz but occasionally win sympathy from the general public.

Notice the flash experience projected in the following paragraph from *USA Today* about a recent contest sponsored by Kentucky Fried Chicken:

> *KFC's contest, which begins today, invites football and fried chicken fans to upload video of themselves doing an arm-flapping "chicken dance" at ShowUsYourHotWings.com. The most creative dancer wins a KFC-catered Super Sunday party package that also includes a new flat-panel TV, limo service for the guests and cleaning team to tidy up the next day.*

If the audience were to Google KFC, they might find this article posted by People for the Ethical Treatment of Animals:

> *KFC suppliers cram birds into huge waste-filled factories, breed and drug them to grow so large that they can't even walk, and often break their wings and legs. At slaughter, the birds' throats are slit and they are dropped into tanks of scalding-hot water—often while they are still conscious. It would be illegal for KFC to abuse dogs, cats,*

pigs, or cows in these ways. KFC's own animal welfare advisors have asked the company to take steps to eliminate these abuses, but KFC refuses to do so. Many advisors have now resigned in frustration.

If you look at PETA's website, you find a list of "victories" from their efforts, including convincing Texas Tech to stop using shelter cats in their experiments; Ad Agency Saunders/Wingo to stop using apes in their ads; and McDonald's to change the living conditions of farm animals that they ultimately use in their products.

FLASH FOR YOU: Should you want more . . .
PETA is an extreme example of an activist group, yet its ability to change not only public sentiment but corporate policy is impressive. If you travel in the activist realm, it's worth examining PETA's strategies, especially where the media is concerned. You can find them at *www.PETA.org*.

CHAPTER 8
Flash! Review

Social networking can be an effective way of getting attention to your brand but can also be slow and time-intensive.

The audience responds to messaging that can tap a sense of reciprocity, belonging, exclusivity, and social acceptance.

Word-of-mouth marketing is divided into organic and amplified. You can use both strategies in your campaign.

You can find in influencers in many pockets of a community, some obvious—such as politicians—and others not, such as popular students in a school.

Integrity is essential to a campaign. Don't invent comments or otherwise deceive the audience.

Buzz marketing requires risk that may or may not pay off in the end.

Negative responses are common in the universe of social media. Do not enter unless you have a thick skin.

9. Short Stacks

The ultimate goal of any marketing campaign is to create the much-coveted brand loyalty. It's the goal of every marketer and the primary reason why they so vehemently target younger audiences and those who influence them. If marketers catch the audience at an early age, they may remain loyal to the brand forever.

When marketers create brand loyalty they are creating muscle memory in the audience. They repeat the action—in this case buying the product—over and over again until they just do it. Musicians, such as pianists, acquire muscle memory by repeating an action, holding their elbows at certain angles or curving their fingers in a certain way. When they play, they don't think about the position of their elbows or the curve of their fingers—they just do it.

However, if a pianist has always held his elbows at the wrong angle, he needs to *undo* the muscle memory. This step requires thought and practice: the body wants to return to what's most comfortable and natural. Marketers reinforce the flash experience through repeated messaging until the audience automatically picks its brand to fulfill a particular need. For loyal brand customers the flash experience has become *internalized*.

For example, when you're hard at work writing, thinking, or engaged in other forms of brain work, you have a sudden craving for a cup of coffee. But do you really want the coffee? Not because you really want coffee in particular but because in graduate school whenever you had an important paper due, you drank coffee. The association between hard work and coffee is hard-wired in you: resisting, even once you recognize that you don't really want the coffee, is frustrating and hard.

In the same way, once a marketing message has become muscle memory, it's harder for competitors to steal the audience away.

According to Nancy Giddens of the University of Missouri, brand loyalty has become increasingly important for three distinct reasons. First, there's sales volume:

The average United States company loses half of its customers every five years, equating to a 13 percent annual loss of customers. This statistic illustrates the challenges companies face when trying to grow in competitive environments. Achieving even 1 percent annual growth requires increasing sales to customers, both existing and new, by 14 percent. Reducing customer loss can dramatically improve business growth and brand loyalty, which leads to consistent and even greater sales since the same brand is purchased repeatedly.

A second factor ties directly to the quality of that loyalty. Customers tend to stick around, remaining loyal even as your prices increase. In fact, they tend to pay more for your brand because they perceive a built-in value—even when your competitors are offering lower rates or sales on a specific item.

Giddens also says that "brand loyalists" are more likely to search for the brand and less likely to be swayed by competitors. "The result is lower costs for advertising, marketing and distribution. Specifically, it costs four to six times as much to attract a new customer as it does to retain an old one."

FLASH CASE STUDY: The Pepsi Challenge

In the 1980s, Pepsi launched the "Pepsi Challenge." The company used so-called street teams to set up little taste-test stands at strategic corners in major cities. There, consumers could "experience" the Pepsi challenge by comparing two unmarked glasses of soda, one containing Coke and one Pepsi—both dark, fizzy, syrupy, and loaded with caffeine. But which one was Coke? And which was Pepsi? Even more to the point: which one was better? Naturally, the advertisements featured plenty of passersby tasting the two samples and proclaiming their fondness for cup "A," which (can you believe it?!) was Pepsi.

Interestingly, although more than half the participants liked Pepsi, the campaign didn't give the company a financial boost. Both Malcolm Gladwell, in his book *Blink*, and Dr. Read Montague, Director of the Human Neuroimaging Lab at Houston's Baylor College of Medicine weigh in on the matter. According to Gladwell, the reason for the campaign's failure was the sugar content. When participants took a sip they went for Pepsi because it was sweeter. But when an entire can was involved, the sweetness was too much and they stuck with Coke.

Montague sees it differently. In 2003, he decided to replicate the taste test, using neuromarketing. He gave the subjects two taste tests. In the first, in which he didn't reveal the beverage, more than half liked Pepsi best, as they had in the original test. In the second, he told the group which beverage was which, and Coke won. The scientists concluded that "All the positive associations the subjects had with Coca-Cola—its history, logo, color . . . Coke's TV and print ads . . . and the Coke-ness of the brand beat back their natural preference for the taste of Pepsi."

In his book *Buy-ology* Martin Lindstrom says, "Emotions are the way in which our brains encode things of value, and a brand that engages us emotionally— think Apple, Harley-Davidson, and L'Oreal, just for starters—will win every single time." In other words, the Pepsi Challenge, good and revealing as it was, couldn't compete with the marketing muscle memory.

To win brand loyalty, the marketer must repeat the flash experience in as many ways as possible. So, marketers engage a number of strategies geared to tap as many senses, trigger as many emotions, and create as consistent a flash experience as they can.

Create a Home Base

In marketing these days, all roads lead to a website. Most campaigns, whether advertisements or tweeted messages, hope to drive the audience to the company homepage. There, they have complete control over the environment, creating the flash experience they want for the visitor. Expert marketers realize the website must be able to achieve these goals. To this end, here's what they do:

TAP AS MANY SENSES AS POSSIBLE IMMEDIATELY

Find videos, music, Flash animation, images, and words. The more senses they tap, the more complete the online experience.

Studies indicate that the audience forms a feeling about a website in less time than it takes to blink. Yet, visitors don't necessarily go to the homepage right away, especially if they're searching for specific subject matter. So, every page must engage the visitor at as many levels as possible.

KEEP THE VISITOR FOR AS LONG AS POSSIBLE

The longer the visitor stays, the more likely she'll engage in the message. In other words, the site needs to be "sticky." According to an article in *212 Solutions*:

> *People have much less time on their hands nowadays. In fact, tracking the duration for which visitors stay on a webpage using special software has revealed that as many as 50 percent of visitors tend to stay on a webpage sometime between 1 second and 30 seconds. So, you have about a half minute to make the visitor decide whether he wants to go deeper into your website. You are in a race against time here . . . .*

GET VISITORS TO TAKE A FOLLOW-ON ACTION

By getting the audience to sign up for a newsletter, print out a coupon, or take some other action, you create a relationship with the audience that deepens their experience . . . and their commitment to the brand. This may also help you track the audience and create a venue for repeated flash.

CREATE A CENTRAL FLASH FOCUS

The audience can ingest only one primary message at a time. So websites have a central focus, usually an image that words, sounds, and other factors support.

Include Search Words Discreetly

The website experience must be seamless and un–self-conscious or the flash experience will weaken. Yet, you must insert words that the search engine will recognize. There are numerous ways to achieve this.

Started in 1996, the International Academy of Digital Arts and Sciences' Webby Awards honor the best in a variety of website categories. One of them is the Toy Industry Association. The name is exactly what the audience will key in when searching for an association of toy makers. That makes them easy to find. Another is Quicken Loans, the company we discussed earlier. Prominent on its website are the phrases "Home Loans," "Home Buying," "Home Equity," and other keywords such as "Mortgages," which are appropriately consistent with the flash experience. The website wording and style project a conservative flash, since most financial institutions won't survive if they're risky, edgy, and hip, particularly in rocky economic times.

FLASH FOR YOU: The Webby Award recommends . . .

Here are some additional guidelines for a dynamic website:

Change your site constantly. Once a week or more add new facts, quotes, updates, tips, or other meaningful content to give the visitor (and search engines) a reason to return.

Include lots of eye candy. Avoid clip-art types of images, especially images of people, unless they're engaged in a task that has movement and energy.

Make your site easy to navigate and friendly to use. Let the experience be seamless and be clear about whether your link is to an internal or external site.

Suggestion: Go to the Webby Awards site, *www.webbyawards.com*, and see some of the award-winners for ideas.

Brick and Mortar

With all their thought about an online presence, marketers can't overlook the flash experience engendered by a physical presence. A strong image, especially one targeting foot traffic, can create a flash experience that leads directly to sales, something other venues such as advertising and social networks can't do. Some businesses manage their physical space better than others. Often small, low-budget businesses can do this as well as, or better than, large ones. One reason is that marketing ultimately leverages innate human dynamics and small business owners follow their gut instinctively.

For example, signs and outdoor displays must create a flash experience for the audience. If the brand entails food, the audience must in some way experience hunger or fulfillment. If it entails sleep, as it would for a mattress or bedding store, the sign must trigger sensations of comfort.

Most storeowners master this well with outdoor displays, offers announced in short, excited bursts, and doors propped open or windows dressed to encourage the right flash feeling. As we discussed earlier, many have signs that engender urgency, using methods including the following.

TIME LIMITS

Deadlines can be artificial, such as "President's Day Sales" or "Fall Specials!" Some simply offer special discounts for no reason: "Two for the Price of One! Today Only!" Reason tells us most will be available for the same price (or can be negotiated) at other times, but the flash experience is not about reason. When businesses hold the sale because they're trying to move merchandise, it's likely that the prices will *drop even lower* after the sale ends.

QUANTITY LIMITS

The flash experience is the same as time limits: urgency. The underlying motivation for the customer is based on the "principle of scarcity." If something is scarce, whether in limited editions, rare, or hard to obtain, we want it more.

The power of scarcity is built into our culture: Parents and teachers leverage it by allocating their praise in small or highly focused doses. Sports competition gets its charge from the scarcity of first-place positions. And governments, school systems, and other organizations unwittingly create demand by banning everything from books to drugs.

When an object is scarce, we have little control over when, or whether, we can have it. By getting that object, we gain control, giving us a feeling of well-being., Marketers exploit the principle of scarcity in retail storefronts, advertising campaigns, and other places.

NEWNESS

By touting a product or service as "new," marketers create a flash experience of desire based on competitiveness, urgency, and even scarcity: the audience wants to be the first to get the coveted object, but they only have a small slice of time to get to the store.

EXCLUSIVITY

The principle of exclusivity is highly motivating for many of the same reasons as the scarcity principle: people are driven more by what they *can't* have than what they can. If the exclusive deal involves a membership of some sort, the audience can belong to a group that allows them in but keeps others out. That flash exists even if the membership (such as a supermarket card) allows *everyone* in. These flash experiences also have an undercurrent of fear: fear of missing out on a deal, losing out to other people, being excluded from a group.

THE INSIDE PLUG

The interior of the store, including the lobby, is a significant marketing vehicle, serving numerous functions. Here are a few of them:

Create a relationship. Marketers know that people are more likely to buy from those they know and trust. That's the fundamental aspect of direct marketing, wherein friends sell to each other in settings including their homes, and the marketing messages are carried by friends and objective associates.

In stores, the sales representative must forge that relationship immediately, so many station salespeople in the lobby to greet visitors, make suggestions, and participate in their decision-making process. The relationship normally deepens when the salesperson argues the customer out of a sale because the store carries an equal or better product for less money, or a piece of clothing doesn't fit right, or the store will have a sale on that very product in a few days. In these situations, the customer is more likely to return and spend more money.

Tap the potential of reciprocity. As we discussed earlier, reciprocity is deeply ingrained in our social behavior. Some nonprofits send unasked-for gifts such as address stickers with the expectation that the recipients will feel obligated to donate later.

Within a business, the principle of reciprocity plays out in numerous ways. Stores may have a bowl of candy or sample for the audience; offer a layaway plan or special coupon; or even have a tab for regulars, who later feel obliged to shop there.

Reinforce or introduce a flash experience. The experience some people have within the store can create a flash experience provoked by sights, smells, lighting, music, and engaging opportunities that transfer onto the product. In essence, the customer comes for the experience of shopping rather than the product itself.

Dr. Ricardo Perez is a pediatric dentist in Bethesda, Maryland. His waiting room has soothing, yet fun, pastel colors, video monitors and a Wii a console for the young patients, and a unique design that mirrors the interior of a cartoon spaceship. The unexpectedly positive design creates a promise that the dentist keeps. The patients can choose from a selection of movies to watch from the dentist's chair, leave with a package of dental gifts, and never see the glimmer of a needle.

Create a "third" place. Marketers know that the longer a visitor stays in the shop, the more likely they'll make a sale. This knowledge has translated into a relatively new phenomenon in marketing, what some call "the third place."

According to Taylor Clark in his book *Starbucked: A Double Tall Tale of Caffeine, Commerce, and Culture,* the coffee company based its model on the cafes in Europe, which are so-called third places. The customer spends her time at home, at work, and at the café where she stays for hours, drinking only a shot or two of espresso.

Starbucks wanted to create a place where the customer can linger, so the company provided comfortable chairs; open, accommodating space; and a design that, although branded, reflected the personality of the region in which the store is located. This differed from McDonald's, the White Castle chain, Dunkin' Donuts, and other fast-food joints whose premise is all about speed: get the customer in and out as quickly as possible and provide seats and tables that are utilitarian but not necessarily comfortable.

As you can see from all this, lobbies are critical to the environmental landscape of the business: the flash visitors see from the sign outside the door or the window display will quickly vanish if the lobby isn't consistent with it.

The Heart Clinic in Rancho Mirage, California, installed a giant, walk-through heart in its lobby, turning an ordinary entryway into a museum. As visitors walk through, they learn how their heart works. The lobby attracts hundreds of visitors each week, including school groups and tourists. It also leverages the clinic's marketing clout: while providing a public service to visitors, the Heart Clinic ignites buzz about the facility.

Other businesses, such as banks, offer coffee and doughnuts to their customers. Some do so once a week, usually on Fridays, while others provide a coffee and tea stand every day of the week. This gesture taps a strong association in the visitor: the smell of coffee and sight of doughnuts creates a positive association of hominess, comfort, and security, the antithesis of the cold indifference of corporate banking.

FLASH FOR YOU: Inside the room

If you want your lobby to attract community members, give them a reason to come back. Here are some ideas about how:

Lighting. Think about softer hues, comfortable lighting, and interesting walls. Stay away from fluorescent lights, as they make people look green and sickly. Use spotlights to showcase whatever will interest your visitor most.

Smell. How your lobby smells can support or undermine your brand. You can use incense or strategically placed cut flowers to generate aroma. If you opt for a coffee and tea stand somewhere inside the room, they'll provide a homey, friendly smell.

Sound. The music will greatly affect how visitors experience the brand. If you live in a noisy environment, you may want to emphasize the noise, for an urban feel, by opening the windows, for example, or squelch it, depending.

Images. What does your audience see the moment they walk in the door, and how does that reflect your brand?

Strive to make your location as easy for your audience to find and access as possible. According to Taylor Clark, Starbucks ensured that its shops were on the right-hand side of the road, so visitors could pull up their cars and run in. The company figured that making their audience cross the street could jeopardize the likelihood they'd come in, even if only slightly.

Create Communities

Marketers work hard to create communities: the underlying concept behind social networks is to achieve precisely that. Promoters of brick-and-mortar operations work to achieve the same end. One of the first to fully exploit the idea was Saturn cars. According to the auto editors of *Consumer Guide*, Saturn created the quintessential community, inviting its 700,000 car owners for a "Homecoming" weekend.

Even Saturn was surprised when more than 44,000 people showed up. All came at their own expense, some driving in from as far away as Alaska and Hawaii . . .

Drenching rains and muddy fields didn't dampen the family-oriented fun, which included plant tours, picnics, a concert, and sharing the gospel with fellow owners and Spring Hill workers. Two employees from Pennsylvania Saturn retailers got married during the event; Saturn President Skip LeFauve gave the bride away, plus a 1995 Saturn as a wedding present.

Beyond great PR, the Homecoming testified to how well Saturn was making friends and fostering customer loyalty. It was judged a success, despite the soggy weather and other problems, and would be repeated in 1999.

By creating a physical community, marketers win the same rewards that online communities do—perhaps more. They're an enormous source of word-of-mouth marketing since community members typically engage their friends. The opportunities for buzz from events like the Saturn Homecoming is enormous. The event helped solidify Saturn's position in the cluttered automotive market. Finally, the community strategy creates numerous other flash experiences, including belonging, social acceptance, and reciprocity.

POLITICS AND PROSE

Politics and Prose bookstore in Washington, D.C., has succeeded in community building on several levels—although its growth was organic and not designed by marketers.

Events. The store has kid-oriented events including circle time, when employees read to the children, and book signings, often with a standing-room-only crowd. The readings are broadcast on CSpan2's *BookTV*, which creates buzz and creates carryover flash of exclusivity, intelligence, and privilege.

Third place. The bookstore has stickiness in part because of the "kitchen space," or café, where people talk, read, eat, and linger around warm smells. It was among the first bookstores to have a café with a "no cell phones allowed" policy. Adjacent to the café is an enormous reading table.

Relationship. The salespeople are knowledgeable about the books in stock and provide assistance and advice.

Accessibility. The store is located on Connecticut Avenue, a thoroughfare for commuters and visitors north of the city. It's equally accessible online: its website has book critiques, podcasts of author interviews, and a lineup of partners who feature Politics and Prose events.

Events

Some brands create events for reasons other than forging a community. The comic book industry is one example. For some time, comic book sales were lagging because of competition from graphic novels and related entertainment. So, industry loyalists decided to launch a campaign one day each year, when they'd give away comic books for publicity.

According to the site *www.freecomicbookday.com*:

> *Free Comic Book Day is administered by a panel representing all parts of the comic book industry: publishers, suppliers, retailers, and Diamond Comic Distributors. Each year, publishers apply to provide comic books at cost to retailers, who in turn give them away for free. Diamond handles marketing and logistics for the event, shipping comics to stores and creating marketing materials and mainstream media excitement.*

And hence Free Comic Book Day began. According to one employee at New England Comics, based in Brookline,

Massachusetts, "No one cared about comic books. They were [a] relic. But all the hype about getting free comic books brought people together. Now we get calls asking about the next Free Comic Book Day." To learn more go to (no surprise!) *www.freecomicbookday.com.*

Here are a few other benefits from Free Comic Book Day:

- It generates buzz. News spreads through organic and amplified word of mouth.
- It creates a ritual, which triggers a flash experience of belonging and social acceptance. The 2,000 participating stores, which include hobby stores, feature comic book signings and people dressed as comic book heroes. Some stores have drinks and snacks.
- It creates a community of comic book followers, which, according to the bookstore employee, has been growing exponentially.
- It provides a flash experience of excitement: limited-time offer, rare or unusual comics, and one-time chances to get the author's signature.
- It targets a clear demographic, primarily of Gen Ys who spend extensively on consumer goods, live online, and so will connect with communities after the event, and use social networks such as Facebook and YouTube to spread the word.

Boom! Bam! Take that, Batman.

Where Online Meets Brick and Mortar

Listservers provide information to a core demographic using more words than Twitter or texts. A private school might have an e-list of alumni and current families, while environmental groups have listservers with updates, action steps, and other activities critical to cause marketing. Since college age consumers no longer rely exclusively on e-mails, they'd be the wrong audience for listservers. Once the list gets too long, it becomes a mailing list in which marketers must get the users' approval before sending them messages. This is an FCC–regulated requirement to discourage spammers.

Quick Hits: Text Message Campaigns

Text messaging is a prime means of marketing to reach an expanding demographic. According to the website *www.textalibrarian.com*, the numbers look something like this:

- SMS text-messaging advertising generates response rates two to ten times higher than Internet display ads.
- On average, Americans send and receive twice as many text messages as phone calls per month.
- U.S. teens sent and received an average of 1,742 text messages per month in the second quarter of 2008.
- In 2008, teens and twenty-somethings were by far the largest users of texting, coming in at 85 percent. In 2009, this continued to be true with teens at 94 percent and twenty-somethings at 87 percent, but usage also increased for older age groups. Among those in their forties, usage jumped from 56 percent to 64 percent, and for those in their fifties it jumped from 38 percent to 46 percent.
- Sixty percent of U.S. mobile phone users now use SMS, compared to 54 percent in a survey conducted last year.

Author and Gen Y expert Ann Loehr says Gen Ys text message profusely, but not for totally frivolous reasons. She contends that the Gen Ys grew up with AIDS, the dot-com boom and bust, and 9-11. They text message to keep in touch and let others know they're okay.

Regardless, text messaging offers marketers distinct advantages: high response rate (many sources say 90 percent of all text message users read their messages); timeliness (text-message users typically carry a cell phone or BlackBerry at all times); and availability (many text-message users rely on texts for information about openings, such as tickets to a sold-out show or new and much-publicized products that just hit the market).

According to Kristina Knight of BizReport.com (*www .BizReport.com*),

> There has been a 10 percent increase of users accessing social networks via mobile devices. That is nearly triple the amount accessing via mobiles in 2007. In the next three years experts predict that more than 800 million users will access social networks via mobile devices; in 2007 only 82 million accessed via mobile.

Although this is a good sign for marketers, mobile social consumers are still more prevalent outside the United States. Currently only about 15 percent of mobile users are conducting local search queries, and 14 percent are conducting generalized search queries. Both categories have seen increases in 2008, with local search growing nearly 10 percent. Finally, these industries have benefited most from text-message marketing, in this order: entertainment/music/video products, food and beverage offers, beauty products, consumer electronics, and travel.

The flash experience from a text message is much like an advertisement or sign in a shop, especially useful for creating an experience of urgency, excitement, and exclusivity.

Let's Text Out Tonight!

The TAO Nightclub in Las Vegas wanted to increase the number of customers attending its events. It tried traditional print and e-mail marketing campaigns, but was dissatisfied with the results. So the club, working with marketers at Club Texting, launched a text-message campaign. The campaign was unique because the text message was the destination of their campaign, not simply the starting point, as with typical campaigns.

TAO developed a simple message: "Text the word TAO The Number 25827 (CLUBS) From Your Mobile Phone to Receive Exclusive Invites To Events at TAO." The club reinforced this message in its bathrooms, behind the bars, on the plasma screens, and on its MySpace account, website, e-mail and print fliers, and business cards. TAO soon generated a list of 2,000 subscribers. Three weeks later, the club text messaged the following:

TAO Nightclub: Tonight—DJ Bob Sinclair with Special Guest Faarsheed!! Ladies Show This Text At The Door To Receive Comp Admission for You and a Guest. 10 p.m.

They received an 11 percent return which, with bar tabs and admission fees for the men, equaled $6,170.

In the two years since they began the campaign, TAO has acquired more than 6,000 members. They text message about upcoming events one to three times a week.

Phone Campaigns

Telephone-based strategies are rapidly becoming dated, but companies still use them. They must create an initial flash of urgency: if the audience doesn't commit within the phone call, she or he probably won't commit at all.

Two obstacles interfere with marketers' success. The first has to do with how the calls are placed. Because less than 1 percent of these calls bring results, marketers make up the difference in volume. To do this, they must rely on automated services. The machine makes the call, but there's a pause between when the recipient of the call answers and the sales representative picks up. That delay kills any potential for flash.

The second problem is the FCC's "Do Not Call" list. Millions of people have signed on and no longer need to deal with telemarketing. Phone marketing, in fact, has such a bad reputation it can drain the power—and flash experience—from the audience.

Direct Selling Campaigns

According to the Direct Selling Association:

> *Direct selling is the sale of a consumer product or service, person to person, away from a fixed retail location. These products and services are marketed to customers by independent salespeople. Depending on the company, the salespeople may be called distributors, representatives, consultants or various other titles. Products are sold primarily through in-home product demonstrations, parties and one-on-one selling.*

With "direct sales" the marketer sells directly to the audience in a familiar environment, leveraging what Robert Cialdini calls "liking." In other words, we buy from people we know and like. Direct sales networks including Mary Kay, Tupperware, and Avon (which also sells retail) sell through intermediaries. When discussing Tupperware parties in his book *Influence: The Psychology of Persuasion*, Cialdini says:

Despite the entertaining and persuasive salesmanship of the Tupperware demonstrator, the true request to purchase the product does not come from the stranger; it comes from a friend to every woman in the room. Oh, the Tupperware representative may physically ask for each party goer's order, all right, but the more psychologically compelling requester is the housewife sitting off to the side, smiling, chatting, and serving refreshment. She is the party hostess who has called her friends together for a demonstration in her home and who everyone knows makes a profit from each piece sold at her party.

As a participant in these parties, I've noticed that other aspects are at work to make the billion-dollar a year industry successful. The experience can be about speed, excitement, and even competition, sweeping participants into a buying vortex. The salesperson (a friend of the host and therefore trustworthy) displays the product, excitement ensues, and the "guests" chatter about the product, triggering swells of excitement and activity.

SOCIAL PROOF

Cialdini discusses another concept, "social proof." Essentially, people do things because others are doing it. This helps explain apparently irrational behavior: Soldiers in World War I rushed from the trenches to certain death along with their comrades. In the 1970s pet rocks and mood rings were popular for reasons no reasonable person can fathom.

Other matters may also be at play: the flash experience of being safe and comfortable because we're with others; and urgency, since the products are on display for brief snatches of time. In some sales events the participants get treated to "makeovers" where the sales representative matches blush, lipstick, and eye shadow to the participant's skin tone and bone structure. The process is so personalized and physical that the participant feels the makeup is actually a part of them. And, quite literally, it is.

We'll discuss more about direct sales in the next chapter.

Online Stores

Online stores work by creating communities, as they make money. Cafepress.com, whose tag is "Self Expression Spoken Here," is an example. In the "about" section of its site, the company tells us:

> CafePress is a community of 6.5 million members, where folks from all walks of life gather online to create, sell, and buy T-Shirts and other "print-on-demand" products . . . . Our Shopkeepers offer over 150 million products—including everything from funny T-Shirts to hats, hoodies, mugs, and more. With so many choices, CafePress is a great place to find gift ideas for personalized gifts and one-of-kind gear. If you can't find the perfect design, simply create your own custom T-Shirts or even custom embroidery. Rewarding self-expressionists since 1999, Cafepress is based in San Mateo.

CafePress also offers a no-money-down opportunity. In that way, it even differs from living room–based direct selling, which charges the so-called independent sales representatives a fee for the merchandise they sell. In addition, CafePress.com includes these services:

- Produces each item when ordered using our unique print-on-demand technology
- Handles all payment transactions including major credit cards

- Ships your products worldwide
- Manages all returns/exchanges
- Offers customer service via toll-free phone and email
- Sends you a monthly check for your earnings on sales!

Of course, Cafepress.com makes a commission on the sales of products.

Street Teams

With street teams, marketers take the brand to the street, giving out samples and, in some cases, engaging passersby in contests and challenges. An example is the Pepsi Challenge we discussed earlier.

Street teams work for several reasons. One is the initial flash response of curiosity, excitement, appreciation, and fortune at being able to get something free. The audience forges a momentary yet valuable relationship with the street team. The flash experience is reinforced later when the audience encounters the brand in a store.

For example, baseball fans typically eat hot dogs at the ballpark. When they eat hot dogs at home later, they experience the flash that influences their enjoyment of the food. Knowing this, some brands—such as Fenway Franks, named for the ballpark in Boston—use baseball as part of their branding.

Here are three examples that demonstrate the range of street team marketing:

HONEST ABE

Berkeley Springs, West Virginia, is a mountainous tourist town with shops and a spring-fed spa, which George Washington allegedly visited. One of the shops, a clothing store and café, sponsors a street team of one: an Abe Lincoln look-alike dressed in a red, white, and blue outfit with a top hat and bowtie. Abe's job is to pass out fliers, which the visitors glance at and then throw away.

When visitors see Abe they have a flash experience of curiosity and wonder—the guy really *does* look like Abe! They are sufficiently interested to stop, take the flier, and chat. Abe has a brief moment to describe the store and café at the corner, but that's more time than most marketers have through webpages or ads. The visitors are impressed with the getup, and the carryover flash is enough to send them to the shop.

A CAVEMAN TOLD ME!

GEICO has an amazing concept for a street team. According to Dean Jarrett of the Martin Agency, who created the GEICO ads, the company set up a kiosk on a Florida beach during spring break when college students were flocking to the shore. On the kiosk was a banner reading "Cavemen are People, Too" reflecting the ad campaign that won special popularity among this demographic. Inside were laptops where students could check their e-mails, Facebook accounts, and so on. While they were there, GEICO representatives strolled by and asked if they'd like to check how much savings they'd get from switching to GEICO. Since they were on the computer anyway, and were under the obligation of reciprocity, they could hardly say no.

This street team concept had many components that made it a success:

- It had a clear, targeted demographic.
- It gave them something they could use.
- It gave them something to buzz about.

- It generated positive and memorable flash.
- It provided a vehicle for the audience to immediately purchase the product.

The GEICO Caveman ads work well because they create a flash experience of fun, surprise, and an insider's sense of belonging (we've followed the ad campaign, so we know the context for the cavemen's anger). The company also sends staff members, dressed up as cavemen, to everything from street festivals to sporting events. Says Jarrett, "Without people seeing the personality of the caveman, it wouldn't work. But the students are in on the joke . . . they're in on the fun."

LUCKY STRIKE, STRIKING BACK

Lucky Strike cigarettes sent out street teams called the "Street Force" to offer coffee, cell phones, and even beach chairs to smokers huddled outside their office buildings for a puff. They even provided them with a toll-free number that reminds smokers that Lucky Strike loves them.

Flash for You: A street team of one

One way to reach an audience, give them a sustained and valuable experience, and generate new clients is from offering training or public speaking. Here are some ways to maximize your in-person presence:

Give them unique and valuable content. If they can find the same information with a simple web search, it's not compelling enough.

Tell the whole story. Don't leave anything out to force them to contact you later. That's disingenuous and annoying—not the response you want.

Focus your talk on one concept or "promise," which you fulfill throughout the session.

Be branded and consistent in everything from your presentation to your handouts.

Have a sign-up sheet for your newsletter or e-list so you can reach the audience later.

Post the responses on your website, assuming they're good. Favor the ones that will bring the ones that will bring the most carryover flash.

Videotape or create a podcast from your talk for your website or blog.

Contact bloggers and other influencers with an announcement of your talk or a synopsis of your most salient points.

Challenges

Just the word "challenge" triggers feelings of excitement, motion, and fun. As part of a marketing campaign, challenges work remarkably well . . . for that reason. The audience is engaged, the flash experience enduring, the buzz potential, with notable carryover flash, immense. To create a successful challenge, marketers have three core components:

1. A highly targeted demographic
2. A goal that serves a specific purpose or makes a promise of a reward at the end, such as losing weight, making money, or bettering the community
3. A challenge that is possible but not easy to achieve

The Special K Challenge, which we discussed earlier, is a great example: it targets women and promises they will lose weight within six weeks from a diet primarily revolving around bowls of cereal. All this plays out in the confines of the cereal box. The marketers create a physical experience in the description of their product, based on the word "crunchy," as in: "Crunchy Rice & Wheat Flakes . . . ." Then there's the other ingredient, denoted in big red letters: "red berries." Actually, they're sugar-coated dried strawberries, but "red berries" has a visceral, sexual quality that deepens the flash experience.

On the back of the box the audience sees a thin woman in a red shirt (creating flash reinforcement) who's smiling and leaning on a doctor's scale, her arms covering the telltale gauges. Hugging the Special K package is a picture of a tape measure, which winds around the lettering on the cover, around the back, and across the bottom—and top—of the box.

This is the Special K "challenge," daring women to lose six pounds in two weeks. It's important to remember that for women, weight loss is connected to a deeper and perennially unsatisfied need for love and belonging. Thin women are sexualized, portrayed as happy and fun-loving girlfriends, mothers, and wives. Heavier women are typically portrayed in the negative: de-sexualized and embarrassing. Some ads for other products even say as much. So this challenge has a highly targeted audience with a profound (and reliable) need.

The flash experience must be tempered with trust, seriousness, and reliability. Hence, the marketers tell us:

Kellogg Company's team worked closely with researchers at leading universities to thoroughly test the Kellogg's Special K Challenge. You could lose up to 6 pounds in 2 weeks. It works!

Combined, the flash experience gets articulate in these lines, also on the box:

The Plan.

The Proof.

The Power!

The urgency and intensity is articulated in the perfectly clipped lines punctuated with the repeated "p's" and tempered with the more reliable "plan" and "proof." The description of the plan continues the excited yet reliable positioning in which marketers tell the audience to "Eat a serving of Kellogg's Special K, Special K Red Berries, or Special K Vanilla Almond Cereal for breakfast with 2/3 cup of skim milk and fruit."

Notice the language in the following line: "Replace either lunch or dinner with the Special K meal." It still merges the flash experience of trust and excitement, introducing a new component, the word "meal." Perhaps nowhere else is the power of flash better demonstrated than there. Marketers replace the reality of eating a bowl of cereal, which at best is a midday snack, with the image of having a full meal. The "challenge" proves invaluable here: should the audience question the legitimacy (or sanity) of the arrangement, the feeling of challenge, of going against their own doubts, pushes them ahead.

Other marketers use the concept of challenge for more upstanding and realistic purposes. The challenges address social issues with a purposefulness that triggers a flash experience of righteousness, pride, and importance. Here are two of them:

TV FREE AMERICA

The nonprofit group TV Free America sponsors TV Turnoff Week each April. As the object of this campaign, they challenge Americans to shut off TV for an entire week. The challenge has been supported by a core group of influencers, including the American Academy of Pediatrics, eighty national organizations, and educators who have spread word of mouth within their communities. Can the students and their families do it? Shut off the tube and not return for seven whole days?

TV Free America's website, *www.turnoffyourtv.com*, supports the excitement and urgency implicit in a challenge with objective and reliable statistics.

The reward is purely social: gratification and social approval from the community including citations from educators, such as principals and teachers, and others. Millions of people engage in the event each year, and 90 percent of them watch less TV throughout the rest of the year.

THE EARTH DAY CHALLENGE

You probably know about Earth Day: the first one sprouted up in 1970. It launched, among other things, the Environmental Protection Agency and helped recycling become integral to our lives.

But Earth Day is only successful because of ongoing marketing campaigns that reinvent the occasion. Most spring from grassroots initiatives, many involving challenges. For example, in 2008, folks in the Syracuse, New York, area were challenged to turn in their old TVs to the Onondaga County Resource Recovery Agency, which received an EPA grant to cover the costs of recycling them. This was part of the larger Great Lakes Earth Day Challenge. The result:

964 cars drove up, bringing 1,551 televisions that weighed in at a total of 97,080 pounds—nearly fifty tons.

Compare the probable results of *asking* people to bring in their TVs to *challenging* them to do so. A challenge is all about energetic language and a physical action: "We challenge you to make the environment better—and break the records of other states in the Great Lakes region. Here's what you can do . . . ."

Challenges also work because they pit the audience against something or someone. This tension is at the core of sporting events, at which teams challenge each other to win a contest, or an individual, such as a runner trying to break a record, challenges the clock. The Special K diet challenges its demographic to take on their hunger.

Earlier we discussed Barry and Eliot, of Jordan's Furniture. They came up with a unique and highly successful challenge that created immense amounts of buzz.

BARRY AND ELIOT REVISITED

Barry and Eliot launched a giveaway stunt that broke all records. The company, as we discussed in Chapter 2, is based in Massachusetts. The people of the Bay State may love beans, cod, and most definitely beer, but above all, they love the Red Sox. The year was 2007 and the Sox were competing against the Colorado Rockies for the World Series. So, Jordan's Furniture launched this challenge: from March 7 until April 16, anyone who bought furniture from the store would get the furniture *free* if the Red Sox won the World Series.

The crowds (and the media) went crazy. People bought millions in goods in the one month the challenge lasted. The local media picked up the story, and then national media started chiming in.

The Jordan's story reached a peak at the end of 2007 when, yes, the Sox *did* win the World Series and the shoppers got their dining room, kitchen, bedroom, and whatever else free of charge.

FLASH FOR YOU: The challenge challenge

Challenges or contests can engage the audience and create invaluable carryover flash. But to pull them off, you need to have a buzz-worthy concept, a dare that your audience can achieve but only with some effort, and a payoff that's meaningful. Keep your eye on the following:

Make sure the contest is consistent with your brand. An Earth Day challenge should not hinge on the success of a baseball team.

Embed the contest in other marketing efforts. Make sure the flash experience is consistent throughout and your core promise to winners is clear.

Maximize your exposure by reaching numerous media, including social networks, influencers, radio and even newspaper advertising, depending on the mix that seems best for your campaign.

Publicize the winner. This will sustain the flash experience and draw additional attention to your brand.

Cause Marketing

There's been a substantial rise over the past decade in corporate charitable giving. For some time, marketers have known that there's a clear link between philanthropy and profitability, provided you publicize your giving enough. This occurs, in part, because the flash experience triggered by the cause will carry over to the brand . . . what we may call the "The Mother Teresa halo effect."

For example, the Seabrook nuclear power plant in Seabrook, New Hampshire, garnered intense criticism from environmentalists in the late 1980s and 1990s. So, the owners of the plant created the Seabrook Wildlife Refuge at their facility, geared to inspire confidence and trust and create an association between the plant and care for the environment. Whether the refuge triggered genuine flash in the vortex of controversy or just won a shrug from the audience is difficult to say for sure, but easy to guess: the shrug.

These days, virtually every large organization has a cause marketing campaign with two components:

- Their own initiatives
- Partnerships with genuine nonprofits

The Home Depot, for example, has partnered for several years now with Habitat for Humanity. According to a press release:

> Habitat for Humanity International and The Home Depot Foundation today announced a national green building initiative, Partners in Sustainable Building. The program will provide funding and resources to assist in making at least 5,000 homes built by Habitat affiliates more energy efficient and sustainable according to nationally recognized green building standards. The Home Depot Foundation is providing $30 million in financial and in-kind support, technical resources and training to establish a foundation of green building expertise that will impact Habitat builds for years to come.

According to the blog site at Alden Keene, a cause-marketing firm, the Habitat–Home Depot relationship is all in the family. Apparently, Home Depot's CEO, Frank Blake, is married to Liz Blake, senior vice president at Habitat for Humanity. That aside,

The Home Depot sets itself apart from its main competitor, Lowe's, and conjures a feel-good flash experience from the audience: "We really *should* shop there."

Several other cause marketing/buzz inspiring campaigns are noteworthy:

AVON

The company, which, as mentioned earlier, now bills itself as "the company for women," hosts the "Hello Tomorrow Fund." If you buy a $3 bracelet, the company will match your contribution until the total amount reaches $1 million, which Avon will then donate to the United Nations Development Fund for Women.

DOVE

The company has a self-esteem project that is part of its Real Women campaign. Among other high-value initiatives, Dove partners with Girl Scouts of America to sponsor Uniquely ME! This program helps build the self-esteem of girls ages eight through fourteen (who also are ripe for brand loyalty) by providing sponsoring programs and other initiatives.

LORD & TAYLOR

The company sponsors a "Buy a Cookie, Save a Life" campaign. If you buy one of its $3 cookies, Lord & Taylor will donate the proceeds to research finding a cure for pediatric cancers. The equation might be off (can a $3 cookie actually save a life?) but the demographic is perfect: mothers and grandmothers who make an association between the department store and the well-being of their loved ones.

AMERICAN EXPRESS MEMBERS PROJECT

You have to love this one. It practically bribes the audience into ownership of the cause marketing campaign. The public gets to vote on which charities will receive some of the $4 million that American Express will donate to charities each year. The company will also "donate" (read: pay) up to $100 person for each person volunteering their time to a charity.

Most of the organizations have the prerequisite social network that allows the audience to join the "conversation." Stouffers, for example, has a campaign aiming to bring families back to the dinner table over home-cooked meals (albeit frozen home-cooked meals). They invite families to discuss how they have benefited from eating dinner together.

Liberty Mutual has forsaken specific cause marketing campaigns in favor of making its entire company campaign, and its brand, about doing good deeds. Dubbed the "Responsibility Project," it involves the insurance giant bringing "Big Issues" to national attention through advertisements showing morally and emotionally trying situations. In one advertisement we see an elderly father, evidently suffering from dementia, sitting alone in a coffee shop on a dark and stormy night. A middle-aged couple, the adult children, watch from the car, quietly wrestling with what to do with him. A nursing home? Twenty-four-hour at-home surveillance?

On the website, Liberty Mutual explains: "Our campaign explores the ways people choose to do the right thing." This is only natural for a *Fortune* 100 insurance company. Right? Isn't it? The

Big Issues range from whether pets should come before people to whether we should watch sports injuries on TV.

Perfecting the Cause: For-Benefit For-Profit Companies

For-benefit companies make money and benefit the world, not as a marketing campaign but as a way of doing business. One example is Paul Newman's company, Newman's Own, whose tagline is "Shameless Exploitation in Pursuit of the Common Good." Enter the company's website and you see the words "Your Friendly Rest Stop off the Information Superhighway." The company explains its mission of donating profits to charities in highly branded language:

> *Newman's Own was supposed to be a tiny boutique operation—parchment labels on elegant wine bottles of antique glass. We expected train wrecks along the way and got, instead, one astonishment followed by another astonishment followed by another. We flourished like weeds in the garden of Wishbone, like silver in the vaults of finance. A lot of the time we thought we were in first gear we were really in reverse, but it didn't seem to make any difference. We anticipated sales of $1,200 a year and a loss, despite our gambling winnings, of $6,000. But in these twenty-six years we have earned over $280 million, which we've given to countless charities. How to account for this massive success? Pure luck? Transcendental meditation? Machiavellian manipulation? Aerodynamics? High colonics? We haven't the slightest idea.*

Countless small businesses have a for-benefit orientation connected to the philosophy of the owner. Liz Gallery, owner of the Stone Soup Bistro, supports local, organic farmers, so she has a 100 percent organic menu and uses local products whenever availability allows. This issue is more of a cause than you'd imagine: in West Virginia, where Liz operates her restaurant, developments are fast consuming land. To buy from local farmers takes extra effort and money, but draws customers in return.

A Little Bit O' Luck

For all the strategies in this book, one factor underscores them all: luck. In the movie *Sex and the City*, Carrie Bradshaw read a book titled *Love Letters of Great Men*. Sales for the book skyrocketed, reaching a rank of 134 on Amazon.com according to the Associated Press. Remarkably, the book in the movie didn't actually exist. But a book with a similar title did: *Love Letters of Great Men and Women: From the Eighteenth Century to the Present Day*. The book, first published in 1920s, has been resurrected and, thanks to *Sex and the City*, is selling well.

Other bits of luck might evolve from less fortunate events. Tim Russert, the newscaster, received an unprecedented number of viewers shortly after his death; more than a year of Sundays combined. A short time after Liberty Mutual launched its "Responsibility" campaign, the economy tanked and large, unscrupulous corporations, such as Liberty Mutual's competitor AIG, distinguished themselves as arrogant, irresponsible, and destructive.

CHAPTER 9:

Flash! Review

To create flash memory, you need a multifaceted campaign, which will probably include some of these components:

- A home, whether online or on the street, that generates a flash response consistent with the brand
- A community, whether virtual, in your shop, or through a campaign that involves numerous shops like yours
- An array of vehicles including text messaging, listservers, and phone calls, depending on the type of message and the demographic
- An online store
- Street teams
- Challenges and contests
- Cause marketing or a for-benefit approach

10. To Market, to Market

As we discussed in the previous chapter, for a flash response to be meaningful, the audience must experience it repeatedly until it becomes flash memory. This entails more than simply replaying an ad or even a series of ads. The audience must confront the brand at every part of their lives: online, on air, in print, on television, tapping as many senses as possible in the process.

For marketers, creating this experience involves numerous strategic decisions.

Push and Pull Marketing

Sending a message is one thing; annoying the audience, creating wear-out, or otherwise alienating people is another. So, marketers must activate the flash response in a constant yet unobtrusive way by using a combination of "push" and "pull" strategies.

Push campaigns are relatively easier for the marketers to achieve: they go directly to the audience, without putting demands on them. The push initiatives must be compelling and consistent, *without* being redundant, and include:

- Advertisements
- Street teams
- Telephone calls
- Search engines
- Events within events (such as booths at a conference)
- Physical locations (storefronts on streets with high exposure)
- Articles about you in a newspaper, magazine, or someone else's blog

Let's focus on advertising for a moment. The audience's engagement is essentially passive. They don't need to do more than see the advertisement for a flash response to occur, assuming the message is strong and targeted. A few chapters back, I talked about the Dove advertisements in the subway station where so-called "real women" with robust, shapely figures posed in their underwear. When commuters made their way to the subway, the advertisement was unavoidable, right in front of them. For some travelers, such as young men, the advertisement may have been curious or simply invisible, but those viewers weren't the demographic.

The main difficulty with push communications is the amount of competition not only from other marketing messages, but the infinite number of other distractions vying for the audience's attention. Think about ads, again, such as the ones in the subway station. The marketer is competing with crowds of people, sounds of the subway, cell phone conversations, and activities such as buying a ticket.

Pull marketing, on the other hand, can be less expensive and is more accessible for small and grassroots efforts. It's also more time intensive. The audience won't experience it by walking along the street; the marketer must *pull* them in, make them active participants in the activity. Here are some pull venues:

- Websites
- Events
- Blogs
- Podcasts and online videos
- Online social networks

Pull marketing creates an interesting dynamic wherein marketers must market their marketing. For example, marketers must generate buzz around a talk or online event that serves as a marketing tool. Advertisements frequently send the audience to a website where visitors can sign up for a newsletter without ever being asked to purchase the product.

Most campaigns balance push and pull marketing. One of my favorite examples is a marketing stunt that People for the Ethical Treatment of Animals launched at the 2010 Westminster Dog Show. The show takes place in Madison Square Garden, attracting dog owners from around the globe as well as plenty of media coverage—online, on air, and on television. What happened, according to an AP newswire service, is this:

NEW YORK – Sadie the Scottie was fully expected to reach the purple podium at America's top dog show. She did, after two intruders turned the center ring at Westminster into their own platform.

The heavily favored Scottish terrier won best in show Tuesday night and seemed to be an easy choice. Her team waited quite a while for this victory—it took a little longer, too, because of a startling protest inspired by People for the Ethical Treatment of Animals.

Shortly before judge Elliott Weiss picked Sadie, a pair of well-dressed women walked into the big ring at Madison Square Garden and held signs over their heads that said "Mutts Rule" and "Breeders Kill Shelter Dogs' Chances," the latter a slogan popularized by PETA.

The effort brought in swarms of attention from every possible venue: bloggers, newspapers, television, and social networks were ablaze. So, you'd think this was a "push" effort, and it was. But it was also a "pull" effort as it drew people to the PETA website. Once there, the pull continued, as the site drew the audience to videos, links, lists, action alerts, and, of course Twitter, MySpace, and YouTube.

Interestingly, PETA denied it was involved in the effort, although it admitted that the organization approved of it.

Balancing the Budget

Perhaps one of the most revolutionary aspects of marketing is that so many of the vehicles are free. Social networks, websites (after the initial launch), online stores, search engine optimization—all of these cost relatively little. In some ways, this has leveled the playing field for small or low-budget organizations. With the right amount of knowledge and time management skills, Mom and Pop operations can compete with the big guys. And, because small businesses usually have a narrower focus and a more personal relationship with the audience, their results can be more predictable.

Unfortunately, many small businesses believe that marketing is complex, time intensive, and difficult to grasp, so they haven't fully embraced their potential. This is bad news on many fronts: small businesses are the nation's largest employer and offer those who have demanding lifestyles (think single mothers with children) badly needed flexibility. Yet around 95 percent of all small businesses close within five years, never tapping marketing strategies that could help them survive . . . and flourish.

Large organizations, caught in an endlessly competitive race, wrestle with whether to fork up big bills or engage in less financially exhausting efforts. The Super Bowl, for example, draws an enormous audience and historically has been the most expensive (and coveted) advertising space on television. Since the recent economic downturn, though, many brands are backing off. According to one AP report:

> TNS Media Intelligence said Monday that 30-second commercials during next month's Super Bowl on CBS are selling for between $2.5 million and $2.8 million. That's a drop from last year, when ads averaged $3 million on NBC . . . .

> For the first time in twenty-three years, PepsiCo Inc. won't advertise its Pepsi brand or any other beverages during the game, shifting its ad dollars instead to a new, mostly online marketing effort . . . .

Marketers in large organizations also confront another difficulty: proving the effectiveness of their campaigns. Too many factors play into success, including trends, the economy, weather, and new products suddenly appearing in the market. Any of these matters can prove to be a tipping point.

So, marketers struggle to find measuring tools. For a while one standard measurement was focus groups, but these have proven to be bogus. Questions tend to be too leading to provide truly useful data. Further, the group dynamic creates social pressure that can squelch dissent or change opinions. Realizing this, some marketers are using neuromarketing techniques, an unaffordable option for most small organizations. In any case, neuromarketing has started raising ethical issues, which promise to rumble up in Congress as well as board rooms soon. Professionals even question the legitimacy of the number of click-throughs, once seen as a testimony of the wonders of online marketing. Now, the thinking goes, up to 95 percent of click-throughs don't bear fruit, whether that's because the visitor was just passing by or because the clicks were rigged.

For now, the most marketers can hope for is to reach as wide an audience as possible with a respectful and artful message.

MANAGING TIME

Timing is a huge issue for a marketing campaign and more complex than you'd think. The audience needs repeated exposure to the message before flash memory sets in. But, too much exposure and the campaign reaches a saturation point; then the marketing effort backfires. That's why big-budget marketing campaigns may run an ad or series of ads and then quickly replace them with new ones. For example, GEICO's ads may focus on the caveman for a short time, switch to the gecko, then move onto something else. The caveman may return, but with enough distance between visits to keep the message (and the flash) fresh.

Marketers also must navigate the muddy waters of holidays and seasonal occasions such as graduations and weddings. If they start advertising too soon, the audience may experience wear-out. Too late, and competitors will have stolen their share of the audience. Further, they must keep pace with the audience's internal time clock. Christmas promotions, for example, draw closer and closer to Halloween each year because marketers want to be ready when the audience's clock says it's time for shopping.

CONSIDERING LABOR

Successful marketing is much like the drip effect in irrigation. Big launches are one thing, but most campaigns must drip-drip-drip the message over time, using diverse and dynamic strategies that create flash memory. Big businesses recognize this factor and develop long-term marketing plans. Small businesses tend to throw out an ad, put up a sale sign, or launch a campaign then wait for the rewards to start spilling in. Without the continued exposure, the marketing momentum ends and the progress—and brand memory—disintegrates.

The reason small businesses neglect their marketing responsibilities can be boiled down to this: who is going to do the work? The business owners don't have time. The employees? They're doing something else. Besides, small businesses consider marketing an adjacency to their primary responsibilities, not a core responsibility.

This is a shame, considering that small businesses know their audiences much better than corporate giants do: they know their customers' names, their kids' names, and their favorite color, flavor, or design. So, their approach can be uniquely, and effectively, personal. Besides, small business owners and their employees *are* the brand, the energy that triggers flash and enables them to launch and maintain their marketing efforts. Here are two examples I witnessed recently:

A wine shop. This shop has an amazing selection of wine and beer, some of the brands dating back 400 years. I suggested that the owner have her employees research the history a little, write up small descriptions of the more interesting brands, and attach them to the unique varieties.

As for advertising: rather than put in the usual 10 percent off coupon, she could have put an ad in the local paper describing that week's feature wine or beer with interesting insights about the selection. The labor was readily available: I frequently found the employees chatting on the phone or playing online games when the store was empty. Ultimately, the flash would be about sophisticated pleasure, perfect for a demographic of retired professionals and faculty and staff at the local university.

A "green" flooring and carpet shop. Although experts, the employees wandered across the showroom floor, asking customers if they wanted assistance. This empty conversation generates absolutely no marketing value. Instead, they should have described the origins of the wood or explained why their green offerings were better for the environment (especially compelling if young children are around) and that they were reasonably priced. They also could have engaged in marketing research of sorts, asking what the audience especially liked or was hoping to find, and reporting back to the owner. The flash could be of quality, social commitment, and style.

For large organizations, marketing becomes its own beast–one way or another. Some firms, for example, have tossed off their manufacturing responsibilities—outsourcing the actual production to contractors—to devote attention to marketing. Other companies maintain skeletal marketing departments, and farm out the rest to large marketing and advertising firms.

These outsiders are hired to create a brand, develop marketing and advertising campaigns, and essentially define the organization in the marketplace. Yet they may not know the client's culture, mission, product, or service except as a spectator. They do know how to position brands so people will buy them. Hence, we have cereals that fight cholesterol, chocolates that are exotic and refined, and software that's avant-garde. Each of these triggers its own flash: trust, sexiness, security, belonging.

The Marketing Mix

Marketing mixes work because each venue affects the audience in a slightly different way, broadening and deepening the overall effect. A magazine ad might trigger a flash response. The same ad on television triggers flash again, but it affects different senses (what they see and hear on TV), by a different process (reading/passively watching), in a different context (their favorite living room chair or in the airport as they wait to catch a plane), with a different set of associations (unwinding after a long day or getting charged up in the morning). The more senses, associations, and thought processes, the more profound the effect.

The movie *Twilight* (and its sequels *The Twilight Saga: New Moon* and *The Twilight Saga: Eclipse)* mastered the marketing mix and created a blockbuster hit from no-name actors and a successful book. The story focuses on a teen romance with the typical beautiful girl and dashing guy who happens to be a vampire . . . the perfect plotline to attract the much-coveted tween demographic. The script is full of romance but not sex, making it a film parents find palatable, if not desirable, for their kids.

The book *Twilight*, one of a series of four, was already a considerable success when the movie came out, having sold 17 million copies to primarily tween girls worldwide. Still, *Twilight*'s success was unprecedented, especially considering the studio's use of relatively unknown stars. Undoubtedly, one reason for the film's success was the producers' unflinching commitment to their marketing efforts. The film cost $37 million to produce. The marketing almost equaled that, with an investment of $30 million.

Another contributor is the filmmakers' insight into their tween girls demographic. These kids are addicted to text messages and online venues. They love to chat. They want to feel as if they belong. And their hormones, much like those of their male counterparts, are raging. So, *Twilight*'s marketers created a mixed-media campaign that consistently addressed this demographic, using the following vehicles.

SOCIAL NETWORKS

Prelaunch trailers went up on MySpace, Facebook, and the You-Tube channel, immediately winning some 4 million viewers. Also, the producers launched blogger outreach through press release, prerelease viewings, and interviews with the stars.

WEBSITES

These ranged from *www.twilightthemovie.com* to author Stephenie Meyer's site, *www.stepheniemeyer.com*.

GIVEAWAYS

Fans who bought presale tickets online from MovieTickets.com or Fandango got a code from iTunes for a free music remix. The physical CD contains a free poster with additional posters randomly placed in the CD cases.

TRADITIONAL MEDIA

Marketers targeted traditional media with the usual pitches and press releases. *Twilight* stars Kristen Stewart and Robert Pattinson hit the television talk show circuit, appearing on Jay Leno, Tyra Banks, Regis and Kelly, *The Today Show*, and David Letterman, among others. Almost every print magazine covered *Twilight*, from

BusinessWeek, which lauded the film's success (before it debuted) to *Entertainment Weekly*, which featured the *Twilight* stars on the cover.

PRODUCTS

Marketers began selling an array of products before the film appeared, including the usual apparel, such as T-shirts, as well as playing cards and movie soundtracks, immediately sparking buzz and triggering carryover flash. The *Industry Standard* reports that the film's soundtrack hit the top of the charts on Billboard, iTunes, Amazon's MP3, and physical CD charts.

Thanks to these efforts, the *McCook Daily Gazette* (November 24, 2008) says the film boasted the second-largest opening for a nonstudio film (*The Passion of the Christ* was first) and more than covered its expenses within the first week, bringing in $70 million.

About Stephenie: Cross-Generational Marketing

According to *BusinessWeek*'s online blog-spotting column, author Stephenie Meyer, who previous to her fame had been out of the social networking loop, got herself into it, spurring her marketing clout. Here's what *BusinessWeek* tells us:

"*Twilight*'s author, Stephenie Meyer, jumped in online in 2005 in a big way on her own. A mom with three kids, she hadn't heard of MySpace or fanfiction sites. But she really wanted to be involved with her fans. She got her brother to show her HTML for the website she created. She spent hours on the fan sites that started cropping up, answering questions. She organized get-togethers online. She got into long conversations over e-mail with her fans. She asked fans to read over her books in progress and did shout-outs in her books to them. The stories were what drew her fans online. But her interaction online helped. All of this helped build word of mouth and loyalty for her."

The *Twilight* campaign has a single tie connecting all these elements (even more than the tween-ishly romantic plot): the flash experience it inspires—one of community, belonging, and acceptance. For example, the marketer's attention to social networks is more than an outreach to demographics: just by showing up on Facebook, *Twilight* becomes part of the "in" crowd. It's important to note that the cachet of Facebook plays a big part in this; when the movie appeared, Facebook was incredibly trendy, much as MySpace had been a few years before. Today the popularity of Facebook has reached the saturation point and its power as a marketing tool is quickly dissolving.

Encouraging the audience to download a YouTube video with *Twilight*-related content onto their own sites creates opportunities for viral marketing. But it also places *Twilight* directly in the audience's lives. It is *their* world, as part of their online identity. Further, their friends see the *Twilight* segment posted there, creating immense carryover flash.

Finally, the giveaways for the film weren't simply door prizes but *experiences*, keeping the audience actively engaged. For example, they promoted advance ticket sales (a common enough practice). When consumers bought them through MovieTickets.com or Fandango, they also got a code from iTunes for a free music remix.

The Bright Flash of Ethics

Earlier in this book I mentioned that most Americans are exposed to 5,000–7,000 marketing messages a day. Cereal companies send them, so do government officials, drug manufacturers, universities, book peddlers, health clinics, psychologists, hair dressers, house cleaners, parent associations, yoga teachers, and religious organizations marketing their orientation to God. This makes marketing the single strongest influence in our society today.

The power and prevalence of marketing means that marketers have enormous responsibility. They must be conscientiously honest, authentic, and clear, not only in their positioning but in the *implications* of their positioning. This may seem obvious, but the marketing world is astute at dodging the issue and tiptoeing over the line between conscientious messaging and lies.

Examples of this abound—for example, in the food industry. Mark Cucuzzella is an Associate Professor of Family Medicine at the West Virginia University Department of Family Medicine and a practicing physician.

He says one way marketers mislead the public is to take a "reductionist approach": if something has *less* of something, then it's *got* to be good for you. For instance, the product Coke Zero is based on the what-I-don't-have concept—it's even the name of the product. The idea of zero calories taps into the consumer's obsession about being thin, which in their minds translates into good health.

But as Cucuzzella, points out, "They may not have calories, but they have artificial ingredients. The verdict's still out on how harmful they are to the body. It's possibly worse than the added sugar." Plus, he adds, what would the consumer be drinking if not Coke? Maybe another zero-calorie beverage like, say, water.

Perhaps the most egregious "zero" marketing advertising goes to Dunkin' Donuts. Granted, doughnuts are the quintessential comfort food and a basic (so rumor has it) of tough guys like construction workers and cops. But a health food? I don't think so.

Then why does the box of Dunkin' Donuts claim the doughnuts contain "0 trans fat"? Because the flash response kicks in—you know, trust, comfort, and all the rest. After all, if they don't have trans fat (which we know is bad for us), doughnuts conversely must be . . . *good* for us. According to Cucuzzella, though, they may not have trans fats, but how about all those other fats, not to mention sugar, corn syrup, and artificial ingredients?

Do marketers realize that they're positioning their doughnuts as something they're not? These are bright people. They're strategists. Their job is to coerce people to take specific actions, and much of the time, it works. Of course they know.

ARTIFICIAL = BAD?

Granted, as many in the marketing universe claim, it's the consumer's duty to check the ingredients list, investigate the brand, and be responsible for her or his decisions. Great idea but, with all the messaging in the world, who can read every label and second-guess every choice? Besides, not everyone knows they *should* read the labels.

At any rate, why lie, anyway? If the brand's any good, just say why it is.

Countless brands exploit the flash response by pinning bold pronouncements on their labels, such as "No artificial flavors," "low fat," and my favorite, "25% less fat." *Poof!* The flash goes off. Marketers *know* it goes off, and the product sells. Never mind that those "No artificial flavors" foods contain preservatives, artificial colors, and modified stuff that has been engineered into food. As for the "less fat"—the question remains: less than *what?* A doughnut that has 25 percent less sugar still has a boatload of sugar.

PRODUCT PLACEMENT

I've already talked about the controversies swirling around product placement. Numerous groups have called for the FCC to mandate that marketers let audiences know that a product place-ment ad is occurring. One such group is the Writers Guild of America. Their president, Patrick Veronne, suggested a "crawl," an electronic tickertape message, creeping across the bottom of the screen every time a product placement ad presents itself at a movie. He thinks the ads, discreetly embedded in the movie's plot, take advantage of unsuspecting viewers and rob scriptwriters of their creative freedom. Other groups have called for the FCC to require that movies with product placement advertisements have notices before the show starts listing the products that are embedded into the script.

The plot thickens when you consider the *implications* of messag-ing, too complex for even neuromarketers to detect. For instance, Mary Kay targets women to be part of its sales force. The company says its "independent consultants" "run their own businesses" and have "boundless earning potential." Yet these women know they're part-time workers, actually receiving commission-only payments for working out of their homes without the dignity of a franchise. That's a situation few men with a family to support would consider.

There are more examples, too many to consider. But, in the end, the best we marketing professionals can do is trust that honesty, integrity, and transparency will be good enough.

And they will.

Good luck!

CHAPTER 10:

Flash! Review

We've gone through lots of strategies and ideas for generating flash and creating a strong marketing mix. So, now it's time to assess your own strategies and see which you're using, which you should add, and which you should pay attention to most. Here are the venues you need to look at:

- Advertisements
- Magazines
- Online venues
- Newspapers
- Billboards
- Television
- Radio
- Product placement

Publications

- Newspapers
- Magazines
- Books
- Blogs

Public Relations

- Press releases
- Pitch letters

- Direct connections
- Radio programs

Online

- Websites
- Social communities (Facebook, MySpace, etc.)
- Blogs
- Podcasts
- Online videos
- Text messaging

Direct Marketing Campaigns

- E-mails
- Phone calls
- Mail
- Giveaways
- Street teams
- Cause marketing
- Public appearances
- Talks
- Training
- Challenges
- Contests

If you want to continue exploring, check out *www.adage*
.com; *www.mediapost.com*; and *www.womma.org*.

Bibliography

BOOKS

Berman, Margo. *Street-Smart Advertising: How to Win the Battle of the Buzz.* Lanham, MD: Rowman & Littlefield Publishers, Inc., 2007.

Cialdini, Robert. *Influence: The Psychology of Persuasion.* New York: William Morrow, 1993.

Clark, Taylor. *Starbucked: A Double Tall Tale of Caffeine, Commerce, and Culture.* New York: Little, Brown and Company, 2007.

Gladwell, Malcolm. *Blink: The Power of Thinking Without Thinking.* Boston: Little, Brown and Company, 2005.

Gladwell, Malcolm. *The Tipping Point: How Little Things Can Make a Big Difference.* Boston: Back Bay Books, 2002.

Hughes, Mark. *Buzzmarketing: Get People to Talk About Your Stuff.* New York: Portfolio, 2005.

Langer, Ellen. *Mindfulness.* New York: Perseus Books, 1989.

Lehrer, Jonah. *How We Decide.* New York: Mariner Books, 2009.

Lindstrom, Martin. *Buy-ology: Truth and Lies About Why We Buy.* New York: Doubleday, 2008.

Rosen, Emanuel. *The Anatomy of Buzz. How to Create Word of Mouth Marketing.* New York: Doubleday, 2002.

Vermeulen, Stephanie. *Kill the Princess: Why Women Still Aren't Free From the Quest for a Fairytale Life.* Berkeley, CA: Seal Press, 2007.

Vileisis, Ann. *Kitchen Literacy.* Washington, DC: Island Press, 2008.

Wibbels, Andy. *Blogwild! A Guide for Small Business Blogging.* New York: Portfolio, 2006.

REPORTS

Editors, New Strategist Publications, Inc. *American Time Use: Who Spends How Long at What*, 2nd Edition. Ithaca, NY: New Strategist Publications, Inc., 2010.

Mori Research. "Consumer Usage of Newspaper Advertising." Vienna, VA: Newspaper Association of America, 2006.

ARTICLES

Gronbach, Kenneth. "Six Markets You Need to Know Now," *Advertising Age*, June 2, 2008.

Higgins, Michelle. "A Plane? More Like a Flying Magazine," *New York Times*, travel section, July 6, 2008.

Johnson, Kelly. "Start Up Makes Cleansers, Signs Up Dick Clark for Ads," *Sacramento Business Journal*, January 2, 2004.

Jones, Sebastian. *"The Media-Lobbying Complex,"* The Nation, March 1, 2010.

Pfanner, Eric. "A Jeweler Joins Its Friends on MySpace," *New York Times*, July 31, 2008.

Walker, Ben. "Sadie the Scottish Terrier Favored," Associated Press, February 17, 2010.

York, Emily Bryson. "Controversy Is Just What BK's 'Whopper Virgins' Is After," *Advertising Age*, December 8, 2008.

ONLINE SOURCES

Alfano, Sean. "Big Mac Hits the Big 4-0." CBS News, August 24, 2007. *www.cbsnews.com/stories/2007/08/24/business/main3200598 .shtml*.

American Express. *www.home.americanexpress.com*.

"American Express Gets Specific and Asks, 'Are You a Card-member?'" *New York Times, www.nytimes.com/2007/04/06/business/media/06adco.html?.*

Associated Press. "Book from 'Sex and the City' Film, 'Love Letters,' Doesn't Exist." *New York Daily News,* June 10, 2008. *www.nydailynews.com/entertainment/2008/06/10/2008-06-10_book_from_sex_and_the_city_film_love_let.html.*

Auto Editors, *Consumer Guide.* "How Saturn Cars Work." HowStuffWorks.com, June 2007. *http://auto.howstuffworks.com/saturn-cars5.*

Ban Billboard Blight. *http://banbillboardblight.org/?page_id=7.*

Bawls homepage. *www.bawls.com.*

Bercovici, Jeff. "Fact: Magazine Readership Is Up, Nix to the Naysayers, 5.3% Increase Since 1998." *Media Life Magazine,* August 28, 2002. *www.medialifemagazine.com/news2002/aug02/aug26/3_wed/news1wednesday.html.*

Bonfils, Michael. "Top International Search Marketing Failures to Avoid in 2010." Search Engine Watch, February 3, 2010. *www.searchenginewatch.com/3636368.*

Boonn, Ann. "Tobacco Company Marketing to African Americans." Campaign for Tobacco-Free Kids, December 8, 2009. *www.tobaccofreekids.org/research/factsheets/pdf/0208.pdf.*

BPS Outdoor Media. *www.bpsoutdoor.com/blog/?p=55.*

Britt, Robert Roy. "Boomers Miserable, Seniors Happiest." *www.livescience.com/health/080416-happy-americans.html.*

"Burger King Has It Their Way with PG-13 Iron Man Cross-Promotions for Children as Young as Three." Commercial FreeChildhood.org, April 23, 2008. *www.commercialfreechildhood.org/pressreleases/ironman.htm.*

Burkitt, Laurie. "Neuromarketing: Companies Use Neuroscience for Consumer Insights." *Forbes Magazine,* November 16, 2009.

www.forbes.com/forbes/2009/1116/marketing-hyundai-neurofocus-brain-waves-battle-for-the-brain.html.

Burns, Enid. "How Active Is the 'Mature' Market Online?" *The ClickZ Network,* May 6, 2008. *www.clickz.com/showPage .html?page=3629395.*

Cahill, Adam, "It's Time for MSN, MySpace, and Yahoo to Pick Fights." February 11, 2010. *www.clickz.com/3636464.*

California Institute of Technology Press Release. "Wine Study Shows Price Influences Perception." January 14, 2008. *www.media .caltech.edu/press_releases/13091.*

Choi, Seoyoon. "Effectiveness of Product Placement: The Role of Plot Connection, Product Involvement, and Prior Brand Evaluation." Paper presented at the annual meeting of the International Communication Association, TBA, San Francisco, CA, May 23, 2007. *www.allacademic.com/one/www/research/index .php?click_key=2h.*

"Direct from Sky Radio—Changes in the Mortgage Industry and Financial Markets and How They Affect You." Transcript of Sky Radio interview with Bob Walters, July 16, 2008. *www.quick enloans.com/mortgage-news/direct-from-sky-radio-changes-in-the-mort gage-industry-and-financial-markets-and-how-they-affect-you-5396.*

Dooley, Roger. "Start Me Up: Brilliant Billboard." Blog. *Neuro-marketing, Where Brain Science and Marketing Meet,* January 20, 2010. *www.neurosciencemarketing.com/blog/articles/interactive-billboard.htm.*

Elliott, Stuart. "The Media Business: Advertising; A Survey of Consumer Attitudes Reveals the Depth of the Challenge That the Agencies Face." *New York Times on the Web,* April 14, 2004. *www .nytimes.com/2004/04/14/business/media-business-advertising-survey-consumer-attitudes-reveals-depth-challenge.html?pagewanted=1.*

Engel, Clint. "If Red Sox Win, So Do Jordan's Customers: Nearly 30,000 Could Get Rebates on Furniture, Bedding." *Furniture Today*, October 23, 2007. *www.furnituretoday.com/article/CA6493340.html*.

Essential U. *www.essentialu.typepad.com/my_weblog/2010/01/the-business-of-candles-soap-ten-digit-creations.html#comments*.

EthnicMajority. *www.ethnicmajority.com/index.html*.

FaceBook Press Room. *www.facebook.com/press/info.php?statistics*.

Federal Communications Commission. *www.fcc.gov*.

Federated Media.net. *www.federatedmedia.net/whyadvertise/conversational_media*.

Follis Marketing. *www.follisinc.com/tagline.htm*.

Giddens, Nancy, and Amanda Hoffman, University of Missouri. "Brand Loyalty." *Ag Decision Maker*, Iowa State University, University Extension website, August 2002. *www.extension.iastate.edu/agdm/wholefarm/html/c5-54.html*.

Harrigan, John B., and Aaron Smith. "Home Broadband Adoption 2007." PewInternet.org, June 2007. *http://www.pewinternet.org/Reports/2007/Home-Broadband-Adoption-2007.aspx*.

Hibbard, David. "Elon Student's Commercial Wins KFC Contest." *E-net Headlines*, Elon University. October 2003. *www.elon.edu/e-net/Note.aspx?id=4430*.

"How Quicken Loans Became a Yahoo! Answers Knowledge Partner." *www.womma.org/casestudy/examples/content-sharing/how-quicken-loans-became-a-yah/*.

Johnny Cupcakes. August 21, 2008. *www.johnnycupcakes.com*.

Jordan's Furniture.*www.jordansfurniture.com/about/history.asp*.

JTLB Media. *www.jtlbmedia.com/text_msg_mkg.htm*.

Keene, Alden. *www.causerelatedmarketing.blogspot.com/2008_05_01_archive.html - ixzz0hndkKHFm*.

Keller Fay Group. "New Word of Mouth Research Finds Moms Buzzing About Brands." KellerFay.com, April 21, 2008. *www .kellerfay.com/?page_id=152.*

Kentucky Fried Cruelty. *www.kentuckyfriedcruelty.com.*

kjerstid "Multimedia in Online Marketing. *www.seo-marketing-articles.com/articles/5727/1/Multimedia-in-Online-Marketing/Page1.*

Leggatt, Helen "Pre-roll Ads Still Causing Consumers to Click Away from Video." *Biz Report,* February 2010. *www.bizreport .com/2010/02/pre-roll_ads_still_causing_consumers_to_click_away_ from_video.html.*

"Levi's Launches Type 1 Jeans." Web promotion, 2003. *www .fashionwindows.com/visualprofiles/2003/levis.asp.*

Levit, Mark. *www.wetalkadvertising.com/8629.php.*

Levit, Mark. "When Advertising Wears Out," *ezinearticles .com/?When-Advertising-Wears-Out&id=8624.*

Linthicum, Kate. "Barak Obama's Text Message Guru Talks to the Ticket." *Los Angeles Times,* January 7, 2009. *http://latimesblogs .latimes.com/washington/2009/01/obama-text-msgs.html.*

"Make a Difference with 'Giving is Winning.'" Beijing 2008 Olympic Games, June 23, 2008. *www.en.beijing2008.cn/news/ official/ioc/n214271980.shtml.*

McClellan, Steve. "Survey: Moms Skip Ads on DVRs: More Than 90 Percent Do Not Watch Commercials When Viewing Recorded Programs via DVRs." AdWeek.com, May 9, 2008. *www.adweek.com/aw/content_display/news/media/e3i80886592 cf59d365473224cf7f661ab5.*

McDonalds. *www.mcdonalds.ca/pdfs/history_final.pdf.*

Mindlin, Alex. "Web Display Ads Attract Fewer Clicks." *New York Times,* Business Section, October 11, 2009. *www.nytimes .com/2009/10/12/business/12drill.html?_r=1.*

"More Women Online: Women Outnumber Men Online, and It's Likely to Stay That Way." *E-Marketer*, April 9, 2007. *www.emarketer.com/Article.aspx?id=1004775.*

MSNBC. "Stewart Begins Serving Jail Term." October 8, 2004. *www.msnbc.msn.com/id/6205192.*

Munger, Dave. "Wine and Taste: Wine Labels Also Affect Our Opinions of the Food We Eat." *Cognitive Daily*, November 14, 2007. *www.scienceblogs.com/cognitivedaily/2007/11/wine_and_taste_wine_labels_als.php.*

"New BlogHer Study Shows U.S. Women Increasingly Shifting to Blogs as a Mainstream Media and Communication Channel." *Enhanced Online News Business Wire*, April 14, 2008. *http://eon.businesswire.com/releases/partners/blogher/prweb857414.htm.*

Newman, Barry. "No Grapes, No Nuts, No Market Share: A Venerable Cereal Faces Crunchtime." *Wall Street Journal*, June 1, 2009. *http://online.wsj.com/article/SB124381591156970663.html.*

New York Times Book Review. "Advice, How-To and Miscellaneous," July 6, 2008. *www.janegreen.com/uploads/bsl_0706081.pdf.*

Nike Corporation. "If You Have a Body, You Are an Athlete." Nikebiz.com, June 20, 2008. *www.nikebiz.com/company_overview/.*

Nike Corporation. "Nike Responsibility, Innovate for a Better World." Nikebiz.com, July 17, 2008. *www.nikebiz.com/responsibility/.*

Nutrisystem. *www.nutrisystem.com/jsps_hmr/home/index.jsp?_requestid=664573.*

Odden, Lee. "Guide to Twitter as a Tool for Marketing and PR." Online Marketing Blog, November 2007. *www.toprankblog.com/2007/11/twitter-guide.*

Petrecca, Laura, and Theresa Howard. "Marketers Go for Super Contests." *USA Today*, December 17, 2008. *www.usatoday.com/printedition/money/20080122/superbowl.*

Phoenix University website. *www.phoenix.edu.*

PR News Today. "PR Newswire Media Survey: Increasing and Shifting Responsibilities, Longer Hours, and Greater Sense of Commercial Accountability Impacting How Media Professionals Do Their Jobs." PRNewsToday.com, March 27, 2008. *www.mobile.prnewstoday.com/release.htm?cat=advertising&dat=20080327&rl=N YTH01127032008-1.*

Ransom, Diana. "Starting Up: How to Network on Social-Networking Sites." SmallBiz.com, March 17, 2008. *www.smsmallbiz.com/marketing/Starting_Up_How_To_Market_On_Social_Networking_Sites.html.*

Roto-Rooter. August 28, 2008. *www.Roto-Rooter.com.*

Samways, Ana. "Ferrit Makes the NY Times." Posted on Sunday, September 10, 2006. *www.spareroom.co.nz/2006/09/04/is-ferrit-faking-it/.*

Shafer, Jack. "The FTC's Mad Power Grab: The Commission's Preposterous New Endorsement Guidelines." *Slate*, October 7, 2009. *www.slate.com/id/2231808.*

Stanford GSB News. "Does a Wine's Pricetag Affect Its Taste?" January 2008. *www.gsb.stanford.edu/news/research/baba_wine.html.*

Stoller, Bill. "How to Write a Great Pitch Letter." Publicity Insider.com.

Sutherland, Max. "False Alarm Theory: How Humorous Ads Work." Blog, August 2005. *www.sutherlandsurvey.com/.../False%20Alarm%20Theory%20-%20How%20Humorous%20Ads%20Work.pdf.*

Sutherland, Max. "Neuromarketing: What's It All About?" Blog, January 2009. *www.sutherlandsurvey.com/Column_pages/Neuromarketing_whats_it_all_about.htm.*

Text Librarian. "Facts and Figures: Mobile Text Messaging Usage in the U.S." August 5, 2009. *www.textalibrarian.com/mobileref/facts-and-figures-mobile-usage-and-text-messaging-in-the-u-s.*

Theblackdog.com. August 20, 2008. *www.theblackdog.com.*

"The Unlikely Titan of Advertising." *CBS Sunday Morning,* February 18, 2007. *www.cbsnews.com/stories/2007/02/14/sunday/main2476130.shtml?source=search_story.*

"Turner, 2nd Firm to Pay $2 Million Over Scare: Cartoon Network Was Promoting Show with Signs That Caused Boston Alert." MSNBC.com, February 5, 2007. *www.msnbc.msn.com/id/16990202.*

TV Turnoff Network. August 28, 2008. *www.turnoffyourtv.com/turnoffweek/TV.turnoff.week.html.*

U.S. Census. *www.census.gov/main/www/srchtool.html.*

Weingarten, Hemi. "So What's Inside Yoplait Yogurt, Anyway?" Fooducate Blog, February 13, 2009. *www.fooducate.com/blog/2009/02/13/so-whats-inside-yoplait-yogurt-anyway.*

Werde, Bill. Interview with Doug Krizner. "Social Fans Support Artists' Careers." *www.marketplace.publicradio.org/.*

Wharton Entrepreneurial Programs. "Take Your Fouls." August 2006. *www.wep.wharton.upenn.edu/gis/article.aspx?gisID=47.*

Word of Mouth Marketing Association. "Organic vs. Amplified Word of Mouth." WOMMA.org. *www.womma.org/wom101/wom101.pdf.*

Word of Mouth Marketing Association. "Student Social Networking Site Builds Loyalty and Generates New Travelers." WOMMA.org, July/August 2008. *www.womma.org/casestudy/examples/create-a-fan-club-loyalist-community/student-social-networking-site.*

Yahoo! Inc. June 23, 2008. *www.yahoo.com.*

Yoplait Yogurt. *www.yoplait.com/products_original.aspx.*

YouTube Advertising. July 14, 2008. *www.youtube.com/advertise.*

Index

sources for writing tips,
137–38
Price
demographics and, 61
as flashpoint, 13
PR Newswire, 132
Product integration, 126–27
Product placement, 122–26, 231
Products, offering variety of,
227–28
Progressive, 33
Pseudo-bloggers, 167–68
Psychology of Persuasion, The
(Cialdini), 156, 160
Public relations, 132–38
case study, 133–34
interactive discussions,
136–37
pitch letter, 134–35
press releases, 132–34,
137–38
text messaging, 135–36
Publishing
of articles, 130–32, 138
of books, 151–53
Puns, in names, 73–74
Push and pull marketing,
217–20

Quaker Oats, 25–26
Quantified
Electroencephalography
(QEEE), 12

Quantity limits, on merchandise,
188
Quicken Loans, 146, 186

Radio programs, carryover flash
and, 139–42
Ralph Lauren, 38
Reciprocity
brand loyalty and, 189–90
social needs and, 156–57
Recycling signs, 7
Reese, Henry, 67
Reese's Pieces, 67, 124
Relationship brands, 32–33, 194
Relax & Rejuvenate spa, 133–34
Remington, Eliphalet, 67
Remington guns, 67
Reviews
advertising, 128
branding, 40
brand loyalty, 216
carryover flash, 154
demographics, 61, 62
marketing, 21, 232–33
names, 86
social networking, 180
taglines, 86
written words, 104
Ridge, Tom, 137
R.J. Reynolds Tobacco
Company, 56–57
"ROFL," 89–90
Rosen, Emanuel, 169, 174